YOU'RE A PRINCIPAL NOW!

What's Next?

TOM HIERCK

ALEX KAJITANI

SHAN JORGENSON-ADAM

RITA MARLER

Solution Tree | Press

a division of Solution Tree

555 North Morton Street
Bloomington, IN 47404
800.733.6786 (toll free) / 812.336.7700
FAX: 812.336.7790

email: info@SolutionTree.com
SolutionTree.com

Visit **go.SolutionTree.com/leadership** to download the free reproducibles in this book.

Printed in the United States of America

Library of Congress Cataloging-in-Publication Data

Names: Hierck, Tom, 1960- author | Kajitani, Alex author | Jorgenson-Adam, Shan author | Marler, Rita author

Title: You're a principal now! What's next? / Tom Hierck, Alex Kajitani, Shan Jorgenson-Adam, Rita Marler.

Description: Bloomington, IN : Solution Tree Press, [2026] | Includes bibliographical references and index.

Identifiers: LCCN 2025030668 (print) | LCCN 2025030669 (ebook) | ISBN 9798893740998 paperback | ISBN 9798893741001 ebook

Subjects: LCSH: Educational leadership | School principals

Classification: LCC LB2805 .H44 2026 (print) | LCC LB2805 (ebook)

LC record available at https://lccn.loc.gov/2025030668

LC ebook record available at https://lccn.loc.gov/2025030669

Solution Tree
Cameron L. Rains, CEO
Edmund M. Ackerman, President

Solution Tree Press
Publisher: Kendra Slayton
Associate Publisher: Todd Brakke
Acquisitions Director: Hilary Goff
Editorial Director: Laurel Hecker
Art Director: Rian Anderson
Managing Editor: Sarah Ludwig
Copy Chief: Jessi Finn
Senior Production Editor: Tonya Maddox Cupp
Copy Editor: Jessica Starr
Proofreader: Sarah Ludwig
Text and Cover Designer: Rian Anderson
Content Development Specialist: Amy Rubenstein
Associate Editor: Elijah Oates
Editorial Assistant: Madison Chartier

ACKNOWLEDGMENTS

I'd like to dedicate this book to John Dressler, my first principal when I began my career as an educator over forty years ago. He took the time to listen, to share, and to inspire all the educators he led. His support was a motivation for many on the team of teachers on that staff to further their own leadership aspirations, with nearly a dozen moving on to lead schools of their own. Thanks also to Aaron Romero, Peter Marshall, and Zenovia Lazaruik, who are all strong principal leaders and who took the time to share some thoughts that helped to make this book even better. —Tom

The most important thing I've learned as an educator is to surround myself with great people. For the book, I surrounded myself with some of the best principals I know. A huge thanks to Holly Blair, Nichole Burgin, Sue Crum, Chris Harris, Sheldon Oshio, Susanna Ramirez, and Kim Reed for your time and expertise in helping us write this book. Your wisdom will reverberate in the hearts, minds, and actions of school leaders everywhere. —Alex

I'd like to dedicate this book to my father, Russell Jorgenson—who taught me a valuable lesson about being a leader and ensuring I work alongside my team rather than directing them from the sidelines—and to Mom, Courtney, and Faith, my faithful cheerleaders. —Shan

To Dan, Leah, Riley, and Colby, with all my heart. —Rita

Solution Tree Press would like to thank the following reviewers:

Jennifer Evans
Principal
Daniel Burnham Elementary School
Cicero, Illinois

Charles E. Farmer
Principal
Freedom Middle School
Franklin, Tennessee

Jennifer E. Gomez
Principal
Orchards Elementary School
Lewiston, Idaho

Benjamin Kitslaar
Principal
West Side Elementary School
Elkhorn, Wisconsin

Aimee Lepisto
Principal
North Marshall Middle School
Calvert City, Kentucky

Lindsey Matkin
Principal
Kinard Core Knowledge Middle School
Fort Collins, Colorado

Michael McWilliams
Associate
Solution Tree
Denton, Texas

Brad Neuendorf
Principal
Lander Valley High School
Lander, Wyoming

Katie Saunders
Principal
Anglophone School District West
Woodstock, New Brunswick, Canada

Bryn Williams
Principal
Coquitlam School District No. 43
Vancouver, British Columbia, Canada

Visit **go.SolutionTree.com/leadership** to download the free reproducibles in this book.

TABLE OF CONTENTS

Reproducible titles are in italics.

CHAPTER 7

CHAPTER 8

ABOUT THE AUTHORS

Tom Hierck has been an educator since 1983, and his career has spanned all grade levels and many roles in public education. His experiences as a teacher, an administrator, a district leader, a Department of Education project leader, and an executive director have provided unique context for his education philosophy.

Hierck is a compelling presenter, infusing his message of hope with strategies culled from the real world. He understands that educators face unprecedented challenges and knows which strategies will best serve learning communities. Hierck has presented to schools and districts across North America with a message of celebration for educators who seek to make a difference in students' lives. His dynamic presentations explore the importance of positive learning environments and the role assessment plays in improving student learning. His belief that every student is a success story waiting to be told has led him to work with teachers and administrators to create positive school cultures and build effective relationships that facilitate learning for all students.

His most recent books include *Trauma-Sensitive Instruction: Creating a Safe and Predictable Classroom Environment*, *Trauma-Sensitive Leadership: Creating a Safe and Predictable School Environment* (both coauthored with John F. Eller), and *You're a Teacher Now! What's Next?* (coauthored with Alex Kajitani).

To learn more about Tom Hierck's work, visit his website (www.tomhierck.com) or follow @thierck on X or Tom Hierck on Facebook.

Alex Kajitani was a struggling new teacher in 2003 in one of California's poorest neighborhoods. His middle school students seemed unmotivated, unengaged, and uninterested in the mathematics he was teaching. Demoralized and desperate, he set out on a journey to turn his class—and his life—around.

Kajitani was the 2009 California Teacher of the Year and a top-four finalist for National Teacher of the Year for the same year. He is lauded for his innovation and real talk as a teacher and leader and is also known as The Rappin' Mathematician.

Kajitani's journey from frustrated new teacher to White House honoree is one he now shares with educators across the United States. He tells refreshingly honest stories of what it truly means to connect with students and colleagues, and he interweaves these stories with proven strategies that educators can implement the very next day to make an immediate impact.

A highly sought-after speaker and a top authority on engaging students, relationship building, and teacher leadership, Kajitani is the author of several books, including *Owning It: Proven Strategies to Ace and Embrace Teaching*, which was named as recommended reading by the U.S. Department of Education, and *You're a Teacher Now! What's Next?*, which is being used widely by new teachers to be highly effective in their first years. He is also an expert of teaching online; he is the author of *101 Tips for Teaching Online*, and his virtual programs and videos are used around the world. Kajitani has a popular TED Talk and was featured on *CBS Evening News*, where Katie Couric exclaimed, "I *love* that guy!" And you will, too! Visit www.AlexKajitani.com to learn more about his work.

Shan Jorgenson-Adam, MEd, is president of JAM Consulting in Camrose, Alberta, Canada, where she works with school divisions in the areas of leadership development, school culture and coaching, and mentorship. She is the former deputy superintendent of the Battle River School Division, also in Camrose, Alberta. Jorgenson-Adam has led literacy, numeracy, inclusion, school culture, community engagement, strategic planning, and leadership development in many school divisions in both Alberta and British Columbia. Jorgenson-Adam has been an educator for over thirty years, working in a variety of educational roles (teacher, school administrator, division principal, director, and assistant and deputy superintendent) in British Columbia and Alberta. Jorgenson-Adam's educational experience ranges from working in urban, northern schools and rural schools with kindergarten to grade 12.

Jorgenson-Adam is a lifetime member of the College of Alberta School Superintendents. Her commitment to success for all students through high-quality teaching, positive school culture, and strong leadership has resulted in marked improvement in several British Columbia and Alberta schools and school divisions. Jorgenson-Adam has presented throughout British Columbia, Alberta, Ontario, and in the United States on topics ranging from literacy, school culture, instructional leadership, and leading learning. Jorgenson-Adam was a key lead on a joint research project on leadership development with the Battle River School Division and the University of Calgary. Jorgenson-Adam has codeveloped two courses for the Alberta School Superintendents association on leading learning and instructional leadership. She has coauthored numerous articles on leadership for the College of Alberta School Superintendents magazine, *CASS Connection*.

Jorgenson-Adam received a bachelor of education degree with a double major in reading and language arts and a master's degree in leadership from the University of Calgary.

Jorgenson-Adam has also completed the Alberta Education Leadership Quality Standard and Superintendent Leadership Quality Standard certification programs.

To learn more about Shan Jorgenson-Adam's work, visit her website at jamconsulting.ca.

Rita Marler, EdD, is a partner in JAM Consulting. She is former chief superintendent of the Battle River School Division, in Camrose, Alberta, Canada, where she focused on instructional leadership development of school and system leaders. Marler has been an educator since 1987, teaching in a variety of schools and courses from grades 1–12. She was also an assistant principal, principal, and district administrator before becoming district superintendent. She has provided workshops and personalized support for school leaders in many different settings.

Marler was an education partner with Education Research Development and Innovation, and was named as one of the University of Alberta Augustana Faculty Distinguished Alumni in 2024 for her contributions to public education in Alberta. She also served for four years as director and first vice president of the College of Alberta School Superintendents. Marler's work has focused on developing leaders to ensure that teachers and schools are improving to help students succeed. She has developed courses about leading learning and instructional leadership. Marler has supported groups of school leaders and individuals in their professional growth as instructional leaders in their schools.

Marler received a bachelor of education degree from the University of Alberta, a master's degree in education from San Diego State University, and a doctorate in educational leadership from the University of Calgary.

To learn more about Rita Marler's work, visit her website at jamconsulting.ca.

To book Tom Hierck, Alex Kajitani, Shan Jorgenson-Adam, or Rita Marler for professional development, contact pd@SolutionTree.com.

Introduction

Becoming a principal is exciting and nerve-racking at the same time. We, your coauthors, remember that mix of emotions when we began our first principalships. This group has over one hundred thirty years of combined educational experience across a variety of roles and contexts. What is our favorite role? Each of us feels the same—principal. However, that experience required a shift in focus from being a classroom teacher to running a school, but we were still able to have daily interactions with the students in our care and positively impact their learning while supporting the adults in our schools to do the same. Anyone who has been a principal knows it is hard work, and the rewards far outweigh the frustrations.

This book seeks to make your work more efficient and minimize frustrations by providing an overview of the key aspects of the position. As a new principal—whether you're leading an elementary or secondary school—you will have at least a few years of classroom experience and a deeper understanding of how schools function on a daily basis. And, though that audience is our main focus, we are also writing for those who have been in the role for a few years. You, too, can benefit from our tools, which can help you determine and work on growth areas.

The concepts in this book apply to new and experienced principals alike because the role is so pivotal to a school's success. Staff work performance, commitment, motivation, and morale are deeply influenced by your leadership style, which includes the following characteristics and abilities (Stewart-Banks, Kuofie, Hakim, & Branch, 2015).

- Approachability
- Communication
- Knowledgeability about education
- Recognition
- Relationships

Cognitive psychologist Eric Solomon (2025) writes about what real leadership looks like. Not surprisingly, it doesn't come down to fear, intimidation, or swagger: "Alpha leadership is a lie. Fear doesn't create strong teams—psychological safety does" (Solomon, 2025). That safety means leaders have the "ability to take risks, ask tough questions, and challenge ideas—without fear of punishment, embarrassment, or being shut down" (Gallo, 2023).

Solomon (2025) goes on to suggest:

> Real leaders aren't out to prove how "tough" they are. Instead, they operate differently:
>
> - They set clear expectations—for themselves and others.
> - They remove obstacles so everyone can thrive.
> - They hold people accountable without making them afraid.
>
> The best leaders don't bulldoze people. They build them up.

However positive your principalship is, there will be times when you think it might be better to stay in the classroom rather than become an administrator. You may also wonder about the following things.

- Do I have the leadership skills necessary to carry out this important work?
- Am I truly supporting student learning in this role?
- How can I do better?

Fear not. No one source can provide all the answers, but this book will provide some strategies, opportunities for reflection, and tools that will support you in becoming the most effective principal you can be.

In chapter 1, we discuss how you can set your school up for success by creating your school's vision. Your vision provides a clear, aspirational goal for the entire school community while guiding decision making, aligning efforts, and inspiring everyone to work toward a shared ideal of what the school wants to achieve for its students. This ultimately shapes the school culture and ensures a consistent focus on long-term educational objectives.

Chapter 2 covers relationships, which the aforementioned research indicates are crucial to your work, showing you exactly which relationships to prioritize as well as how to approach and build real connections within your school and the wider community. New principals often believe they have to first build relationships and then do the other work. However, it is important to remember that strong, trusting relationships are built *while* you are doing the work.

Because communication is an important aspect of your work as a principal, chapter 3 looks at effective methods and tools that support your leadership work and help ensure you are in control of your school's narrative.

Chapter 4 explores school culture. This aspect of school leadership can be eye opening for a new principal. As classroom teachers, we often think that everyone feels the same about the school and works the same way. Visiting a teacher's classroom as a principal and learning about how things in your new school really work can be a shock. In this chapter, we provide ideas and examples of how you can build a school culture that focuses on a safe and welcoming learning environment.

Research shows that, next to the classroom teacher, principals have the greatest impact on student learning (Allensworth & Hart, 2018; Robinson, 2011). How do you generate this impact? It comes from your instructional leadership practices. In chapter 5, we look at some key aspects of instructional leadership that are vital to your success as a new principal. We also provide strategies and resources for you to use.

As a teacher, you focus on your own professional learning. As a principal, you still focus on your own professional learning, but you also support your staff and stakeholders. In chapter 6, we provide strategies, resources, and structures you can use to support both your own and others' professional learning. We also look at the important topic of self-care and how you can maintain a healthy work-life balance.

The good news is that you have many people in your school community who have leadership skills and can support you in all aspects of your leadership work. Chapter 7 provides you with advice on how to support and build leadership skills in others. We also provide ideas and strategies on how to do this work and how you can benefit from it.

Chapter 8 looks at the management aspects you are responsible for as a principal. Be warned that many new principals let this part of the job become front and center. We believe that prioritizing and leveraging other school leaders can ensure that your management tasks are completed and your instructional leadership work can still be the priority.

Throughout this book, you will find real-life stories of the great work principals are doing in schools. We share strategies, structures, resources, and tools you can use to support you in your new role. Chapters include Tips to Thrive sections containing additional ideas and strategies from real principals who, like you, are working to ensure high-quality learning for the students in their care.

There is no argument that being a principal is a big responsibility and requires someone who is not afraid of hard work. The good news is that you are not alone. There are others, like us, who want to support your success because we know you can make a difference.

Chapter 1 How Do I Develop Vision?

Before diving in, take a moment to reflect on how you got here. The things you've accomplished, the relationships you've built, and the skills you've acquired have all played a pivotal role in establishing you as your school's leader. By the end of this chapter, you'll be able to communicate the vision that you have for your school. But before that, contemplate the following questions.

- What accomplishment are you most proud of as an educator?
- What do you hope people will say when they talk about you as a teacher (or whatever your role was before becoming a school administrator)?
- What do you feel like you haven't accomplished in the work you've done?

Reflecting on your answers is important because they'll help you identify the strengths you've built, which will help you transition into leading your school. The last question also helps you identify growth areas. Keep these questions and your responses close at hand as you work toward your vision. You may find guidance in them, and your responses may shift as your vision gets clearer.

Vision is often misunderstood and frequently entwined with the concept of mission. It's important to separate these two concepts. At the simplest point of clarification, *mission* speaks to the present (what a school is doing today), while *vision* speaks to the future (what the school hopes to achieve or become). As you think of your role as a leader, your *personal* vision will help influence the vision for your school, but we suggest you exercise caution so your vision doesn't become the school's vision. As middle school principal Aaron Romero shares, "My vision is representative of who I am as an educator and the lengths to which I will go to best meet the needs of the students that I serve" (personal communication, February 22, 2025).

While considering your personal vision and expectations, it may be helpful to think forward and envision yourself as that successful leader you plan to become. Educator Peter Marshall (2025) suggests that you might imagine asking your future self, "How did your daily interactions with staff, students, and families in your community illustrate to them that the role of school administrator is important and rewarding . . . ?" (p. 1).

We would add to this: How might achieving clarity of your personal vision help you lead your team through a visioning exercise? Understanding your strengths, as well as your growth opportunities, is a good starting point.

- **Your strengths:** What are your strengths? There are a variety of tools that could assist you in identifying these; however, you probably already have a good idea of what your strengths are. You may have even leveraged these during the interview process that landed you your new job. How have these strengths shaped your personal vision?
- **Your growth opportunities:** Potentially even more important is identifying your growth opportunities. Notice we did not use *weaknesses* to indicate the opposite of strengths. Our lived experiences highlight the significance of language. *Weakness* tends to acknowledge an acceptance of a deficit, while *growth opportunity* suggests a desire to improve in that area. This does not mean that these areas will become strengths, but it does speak to a desire to improve and the efforts and actions you take to grow. Think of the powerful message it sends to a school when its leader is both aware of their gaps and willing to address them.

Before looking at those strengths and growth opportunities, consider those of the job itself and how your own strengths and growth opportunities overlap.

Growth opportunities appear in the following list.

- **It can be stressful:** Principals often work under pressure because they handle stress-inducing things like managing the school's budget, making staffing decisions, and ensuring students succeed in achieving the desired outcomes. Making these important decisions and taking accountability for any obstacles that emerge can be taxing.
- **You will work long hours:** Principals often work more than fifty hours each week, even working in the evenings or on some weekends. A 2018 report suggests that the average time a principal works is sixty-one hours per week (Fuller, Young, Richardson, Pendola, & Winn, 2018), so be prepared for that. You will likely even work during school breaks. The hours when school is in session are spent interacting with your students, staff, families, and your community—people time. The hours *after* school are paper time. It would be disingenuous of us to suggest the workload will lighten when you have greater control of the school's direction.
- **You will help resolve many conflicts:** As a principal, you might spend a lot of your day resolving conflicts. These disagreements can involve students, teachers, parents, or guardians. If you handle stress well and enjoy finding solutions to interpersonal problems, this aspect of the role might be a strength rather than a growth opportunity. It's likely you will be heavily involved with student discipline. While some professionals might find this part of the role unpleasant, you can view discipline as the teaching required to function in

accordance with the school's expectations. Consequence paired with instruction can help prepare students to be successful adults (Alliance for Resource Equity, n.d.). Discipline often leads to difficult conversations with students and their parents, so it's important to engage in these discussions with empathy while maintaining the expectations of the school.

Strengths appear in the following list.

- **You can have a positive impact on students:** Principals have a positive impact on students' academic success, their sense of belonging, and their futures because they work directly with them.
- **You can influence school culture:** Principals get to make some decisions that help define the culture of the school both today and into the future. Principals strongly influence schoolwide expectations and policies, events and activities, hiring, and many more decisions that shape the culture.
- **There's variety in your daily tasks:** Principals handle new issues every day because there are often new obstacles to solve or projects to monitor. While the typical responsibilities—like evaluating teachers and working with the school's budget—demand time and focus, there are many more community-building opportunities to focus on.
- **There are many leadership opportunities:** Principals get the opportunity to practice leadership skills every day. New teachers may look to the principal for guidance when developing their teaching strategies and learning the ropes of their new role. Veteran teachers may seek mentorship as they contemplate their own career options. Additional mentoring may occur with an assistant principal or vice principal who works alongside them.

As you gain clarity on your strengths and growth opportunities, use that clarity to refine your personal vision and help you build your leadership team. The members of a leadership team could vary depending on your school size, but may include your assistant principals, department heads, instructional coaches, counselors, and librarians. While the temptation may be to form a team of like-minded individuals, your vision could become narrow and the richness of these varied strengths could be lost.

As this chapter introduction comes to an end, consider the question posed by principal Baruti K. Kafele (2019) in the title of his book *Is My School a Better School Because I Lead It?* This is an excellent way for new leaders to reflect on the role they're starting. Perhaps jot down your thoughts on an index card, keep it close, and use it to check on your personal growth and accomplishments.

After developing your personal vision, you will distinguish commitment from buy-in, help lead your team's vision creation, and believe that all students will learn.

Distinguish Commitment From Buy-In

First, a leader must distinguish commitment from buy-in. In our experience, leaders often interchange the ideas of commitment and buy-in, but we assert these are *not* the same thing. Buy-in tends to be surface-level agreement that signifies acceptance. Commitment, however, runs deeper. It requires belief in what you're doing.

Leaders are often happy to achieve buy-in. Buy-in tends to be a logical decision that is arrived at after weighing the alternatives and hearing the rationale. It may even be an act of support for a highly regarded leader, but we're not convinced it leads to an organization's long-term success or the long-term viability of its vision. Commitment, however, speaks to a strong belief in the vision—a desire to own the vision and to carry it forward. It's not an act of compliance—even if that is borne from positive intent—but instead it is something beyond a logical decision or support for a preferred leader. It is more of a complete investment combining both logic (the head) and emotion (the heart). The difference between buy-in and commitment might make all the difference in a school's success.

A wide range of students will enroll in your school, and all students will need to be welcomed with inclusion and empathy as you, the school leader, create an environment in which they can learn and grow safely. This is clearly beyond the scope of buy-in, and everyone's success will rest on how committed your team is to the vision. Stopping at buy-in is not likely your best leadership launching pad. Commitment sets the wheels in motion for you to lead your team on a systemwide journey. For most schools, the difference between buy-in and commitment might make all the difference in a leader's ability to successfully sustain their efforts.

Help Lead Your Team's Vision Creation

You may be wondering why a vision statement is so important for the team you'll lead. A vision statement describes your team's loftiest ideas, core values, long-term objectives, and what students should learn or be capable of doing after their schooling years are finished. Creating this vision may begin with an activity as simple as asking each person to share a word or sentence describing what they feel is the most important thing about the school they work in. Often, these initial thoughts are the beginnings of a broader mission. Themes like collaborative, cooperative, focused, welcoming, supportive, and knowledgeable can readily form the basis of your vision. This is more than a collection of fifty-cent words. At its core, your team's vision is an organizational compass, motivator, and strategic tool.

Because schools communicate their vision and mission frequently and in highly visible spots in the school—and on websites, newsletters, and meeting agendas—we've included some real-world vision statement examples. You can always use these examples to start the work and then build your own mission and vision through dialogue with your staff and student families.

Falun Elementary School in Falun, Alberta, Canada states:

> We envision a school in which members:
>
> - Create a system of timely interventions and extensions based on evidence to ensure academic success
> - Maintain effective communication within our educational community
> - Collaboratively and intentionally establish schoolwide relationships, the pillar of our learning community
> - Demonstrate a personal commitment to the growth of productive global citizens (Wetaskiwin Regional Public Schools, n.d.)

Nellie McClung School (n.d.) in Calgary, Alberta, Canada states:

> At Nellie McClung, we strive to have all learning community members:
>
> - Actively involved in the learning process
> - Demonstrate respect for self and others
> - Accept responsibility for our roles within the community

American Senior High School (n.d.) in Hialeah, Florida states:

> The vision of American Senior High School is to inspire and prepare our students for a competitive global community. We will instill in them critical thinking skills, a desire for learning, and a respect for the core values of integrity, compassion, and perseverance.

Schools should have a vision statement because it provides a clear, aspirational goal for the entire school community while guiding decision making, aligning efforts, and inspiring everyone to work toward a shared ideal of what the school wants to achieve for its students. Goal setting like this does impact behaviors (Epton, Currie, & Armitage, 2017). Ultimately, a vision should shape a school's culture and ensure a consistent focus on long-term educational objectives:

> One of the most concrete ways vision statements affect schools is by helping to inform decision making. Between teachers, students, families, and administrators, there are naturally a lot of different opinions. Discussions surrounding resource allocation or policymaking often result in gridlock. With a solid vision statement, however, you can refocus on shared goals and values. This can provide helpful rationale when working through tough decisions. (University of Massachusetts Global, 2020)

Kenneth C. Williams and Tom Hierck (2015) identify three levels of visioning that align perfectly with the move from buy-in to commitment: (1) inspiration, (2) aspiration, and (3) perspiration. You will take your team through this natural progression as you work on creating your vision and then work toward it.

Inspiration

An inspiring vision rallies individuals to a greater purpose, even if it seems daunting at first. We have to do more than convince or guilt educators into being their best. An inspiring and shared vision can be a galvanizing force when we understand what motivates people. This is the start of the move toward commitment.

Contemplate the following questions about your school's image with the team that is creating the vision.

- What image do you have in your mind of our school?
- What is the image the district has of our school?
- What is the image the community has of our school?
- Are these images that we want to represent our school?

As you respond to these questions, keep in mind that *someone* is crafting an image of your school. It may not be the image you or your team wants; it may not even be an accurate one. Unless you and your team craft the image based on the realities of your school's daily life, the picture will be incomplete at best and inaccurate at worst. What inspires you to come to work each day? What inspires your team and your students?

The inspiration level is important for achieving commitment, but a major reason visioning is so underused in school cultures is because schools rarely move past the inspiration level of vision. We often encounter schools that both *start* and *stop* at being inspired. They typically find themselves back in a rut with their efforts needing to be reenergized and team members needing to recommit.

Aspiration

Once your team has a shared understanding and is engaged and ready to work, you move to the second level—aspiration. The work at this level aims to identify (or reconnect with) the essential work required to become the ideal school.

Your personal vision, which you crafted as the school leader, may assist you in shaping this next step. What have you seen that produced results aligned with your personal vision? What leadership skills helped move teams forward? Remember, you might need to clarify the difference between a *best practice* and the *practice you are best at.* These might not be the same thing. Reflecting on best practices should reveal areas where your school is strong, as well as opportunities for learning, growth, and improvement.

Contemplate the following scenario with your team: You open the newspaper five years from now and are reading about your school. What does the headline say? Reflecting on this can help your team develop a vision of what they aspire to create and build shared knowledge of what is needed to get there. This is getting your team on the verge of necessary, deeply entrenched commitment.

You will lead conversations about potential vision concepts. For example, if the vision crafted was "all students will learn," or included notions like equity or success, the leader must ensure all voices are heard.

Achieving commitment to a vision statement requires a vision-creating team to do three things.

1. Clarify the meaning of the word.
2. Accommodate individual views of the word and ensure that the word's definition is agreed on going forward.
3. Ensure that future products are not the result of a voting process. (In other words, if a passionate view is held, we can't expect the passion to fade because they were on the wrong side of the vote. Consensus building is an absolute.)

This work will never be about finding the perfect words but about ensuring that variations in how the word is understood are considered and a common understanding is achieved. As an example, consider the word *summarize.* Would your definition contain "to give the key points," "make shorter," "main points," "a brief statement," or "recap"? None of these are incorrect, but they each represent a different shade of gray that requires the team to fully understand what the term means before including it.

Perspiration

This final, critical stage allows you and your staff to evaluate areas in which team members must build shared knowledge. You have to build knowledge of what it takes to achieve the vision. Commitment takes root when staff members have absolute clarity on expected best practices and on specific observable behaviors and protocols embedded in each of those practices.

As a team, contemplate this question: What must we do so that staff can assess their strengths and growth opportunities, learn together, and move ahead as a learning community?

The perspiration level is essential for moving from buy-in to commitment. This is hard work. That's what causes perspiration, and unfortunately, some teams cannot get to that point and stall (or are too intimidated to try).

Believe That All Students Will Learn

Read the heading to this section again. Did you notice it says *all* and *will*? Learning for all is not something to hope for. It should be the mission of every school on behalf of every student. If learning is not the single most important outcome and desire, what is? If this outcome is contingent on external factors like better students, better parents, better funding, and so on, then you don't really have a vision of success. You have something you're hoping for.

Don't get us wrong. We fully understand that factors external to the school can have an impact, but they should not be used as a rationale for lack of performance or achievement. Leaders must believe that they and their team have the talent and capacity to guarantee learning for all students. As a leader, you demonstrate the unrelenting focus and positive mindset that lead your team to believe that the vision is attainable. Positive-attitude author Jon Gordon (2017) has a great perspective on this:

> Positive leadership is not about fake positivity. It is the real stuff that makes great leaders great. Pessimists don't change the world. Critics write words but they don't write the future. Naysayers talk about problems but they don't solve them. Throughout history we see that it's the optimists, the believers, the dreamers, the doers, and the positive leaders who change the world. (p. 9)

Remind your team that hard moments often define us. How do they view challenges? Do they use them as stumbling blocks or as stepping-stones? When struggles occur, will team members turn, look each other in the eye, and say, "We got this!" or will they turn away from each other? If you, as the leader, remain firm and support team members during moments of doubt, these moments can help solidify the ownership of the vision and your school's commitment to it.

Every student who is fortunate to join you and your team at your school has their own unique attributes. You will have gathered information and evidence on every student. In fact, one of the key roles of school leaders is to know every student by name and by need. Once you have this information, there is a significant question you and your team must confront: Are we gathering information to make plans or to make excuses?

Making plans means we understand the unique nature of each student, and we design a school experience that leads them to be functional adults who can make valuable contributions to their communities. Making excuses, on the other hand, means we limit the student's potential and lower our expectations, potentially limiting their future capacity. The information gathering takes the same amount of time. The response is where we decide if we have buy-in or commitment, inspiration or perspiration. As goes the leader, so goes the team. As author Jay Jackson (2023) suggests, "Self-awareness is the foundation of character performance. It is where we begin to see ourselves as we truly are, so we can identify where we have space to grow" (p. 12).

Final Thoughts: Evolve Hopes and Aspirations Into Vision

At the start of this chapter, you contemplated three questions. Let's revisit them here so you can jot down some thoughts now that you've read and processed this chapter.

- What accomplishment are you most proud of as an educator?
- What do you hope people will say when they talk about you as a teacher (or whatever your role was before becoming a school administrator)?
- What do you feel like you haven't accomplished in the work you've done?

As you consider your responses to these questions and the significance of your new role in leading your team, the words of veteran principal Zenovia Lazaruik may provide a sense that the work is doable, necessary, and undeniably valuable: "A vision paints a vivid picture of our aspirations, illuminating the path toward our goals and serving as a compass for our journey. It helps us prioritize our most significant objectives" (personal communication, March 11, 2025).

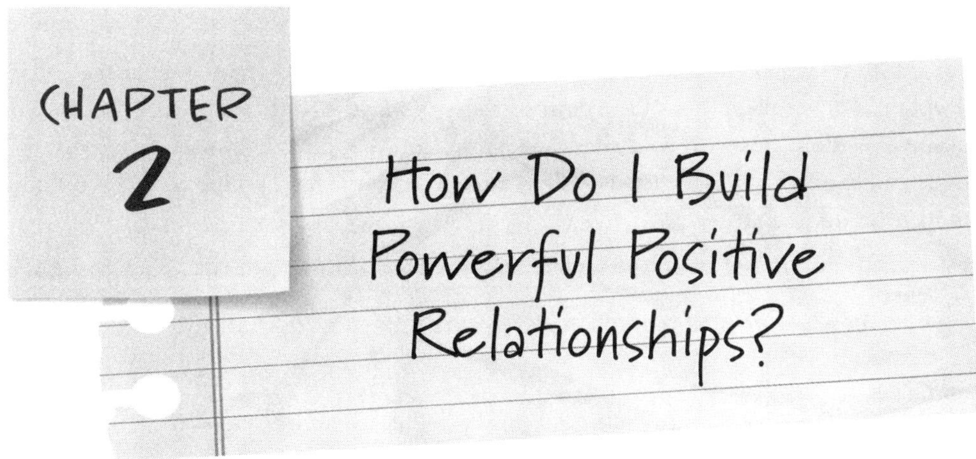

Chapter 2: How Do I Build Powerful Positive Relationships?

As a principal, your relationships will play a key role in determining your successes or growth opportunities as a leader. How people feel about you will often translate into how they feel about the entire school and even the education system, but don't let that intimidate you. You've got this! This chapter shows you exactly which relationships to prioritize, as well as how to approach and build real connections within your school and the wider community.

Let's start with two simple questions.

1. **What is a relationship?** Relationships are connections. As a principal, you are the leading force for all the relationships that exist within your school community. Each day is an opportunity to grow and strengthen these connections so that everyone thrives. Along with growing and strengthening relationships, be mindful of not letting them stagnate.
2. **What relationships should a principal prioritize building?** It sounds like a lot, but *all* relationships are important. Every stakeholder—from the students who attend your school to the board members who make critical decisions about it—will form much of their opinion about your school based on their relationship with you. Every positive relationship you build is an opportunity to impact the work you are doing and to impact their opinions of that work.

Here are the most common groups you'll need to build relationships with.

- Teachers and staff
- Students
- Parents and guardians
- District-level administrators
- Your site leadership team
- Community members

As you read further, notice there are overlapping themes among these groups, which can become part of your overall approach to relationship building as a principal.

For example, when you build a positive relationship with a parent or guardian, that deeply impacts the quality of the connection you have with their child. As you build positive relationships with your site leadership team, that directly improves the connections you have with those teachers. Then, each group has a few specific elements unique to its role and yours.

Table 2.1 explains some of the nuances between teacher and principal relationships.

Table 2.1: Teacher and Principal Relationship-Building Differences

As a Teacher	As a Principal
You build relationships with the teachers you work alongside the most, such as those in your department or grade level. Principal turnover negatively impacts teacher job satisfaction (Grissom, Egalite, & Lindsay, 2021).	You build relationships with teachers and staff members who will hopefully return each year, often over several years. You understand that it can be disheartening to teachers to have a new principal—especially a new one each year.
You build new relationships with students in your class, and often their families, each year. At the end of the school year, they usually move on to another teacher or school. You tend to see your students the same amount each day.	You build new relationships with students and their families from all grade levels each year as they enter your school. At the end of the school year, they may stay, or they may move on to another school. You tend to see the more visible students and families more often than some of the others.
You may not have much interaction with your district superintendent.	You regularly communicate with your district superintendent.
You mostly interact with your school's leadership team at meetings and outside of class.	You interact with your school's leadership team to plan meetings and, often, while the teachers are in their rooms with students.
You may not have much interaction with community members, and they are rarely in your classroom.	You have much interaction with community members, and they are an important part of the work you do as the school's leader.

Build Relationships With Teachers and Staff

When it comes to the success of a single classroom, nothing is more important than the relationship between the teacher and their students. And when it comes to the success of an entire school, nothing is more critical than the relationship among the adults in the building. Research proves that "social interactions among educators are vital to productive learning climates, both in terms of student learning and teachers' professional development" (Price & Moolenaar, 2015).

If you are new to a building or new to the role of principal, it is essential that you set up meetings with teachers and staff before the school year begins. You can start during preservice days at the beginning of the year or even before that. Depending on how much time and how many staff members you have, you can set up half-hour meetings for each individual or for small groups.

As principal, each day is an opportunity to strengthen the relationships among your staff—starting with each staff member's relationship *with you*. While building relationships is a critical first step, *maintaining and strengthening those relationships over time* will help you and your school community reach true success.

You don't necessarily need to *build* the relationships first in order to do the work. Often, doing the work leads to building the relationships, which leads to doing more great work! Renowned educational researcher Viviane Robinson finds that when school leaders focus on engaging in the daily work with colleagues, trust builds naturally, and strong relationships grow along the way. According to Robinson (2011), "Leadership that is focused on improving teaching and learning will, over time, build the relational trust that is necessary for effective collaboration" (p. 132).

The following strategies help you build, maintain, and strengthen relationships with your teachers and staff.

- Meet individually or in small groups.
- Be visible.
- Include teachers in the planning.
- Know the contract.
- Start with the interview.

Meet With Your Teachers and Staff Individually or in Small Groups

While it may seem like meeting with every staff member individually is going to be quite time consuming, it will also be one of the best investments of time you can make. Try setting aside a specific time each day (like thirty minutes in the morning or after school) to meet with staff members. This includes the custodial staff in your building, since they are integral to ensuring a safe environment and can be instrumental in creating the conditions where staff and students feel cared for. Your administrative assistants and assistant principals can be your greatest allies if you start the year off on a good note.

If meeting with everyone individually is going to take way too long, consider meeting with them in small groups or two or three at a time. This allows you to meet with more people over a shorter amount of time. Plus, watching how certain staff members interact with each other will give you helpful insights into everyone's personalities! When you meet, share your vision for the school, as well as the best ways and times to contact you. You should also share something about your own life to help them get to know you a bit.

Here are several questions that will get to the heart of who they are as members of your staff. You probably won't have time to get through all of these questions, so pick those that matter the most to you.

- What is most important to you about this school?
- What do you most want me to know as the incoming principal?
- What has gone well in the past?
- What areas need improvement or are concerning to you?
- What personal information would you like to share, if any?
- What is one thing you would change or improve at this school?
- How did you come to work at this school?
- How is your time best spent during staff development?
- How would you describe the culture here?
- What are you looking for from me as your principal?

These meetings allow you to get to know everyone on your staff individually and allow them to feel seen. Be sure to take a few notes so you can remember and refer to some of the things you learn about your colleagues as the year rolls on. (Everyone likes to know that their boss remembered what they talked about and are impressed when you bring it up later.)

Stop, start, continue is another strategy you can use, especially if you won't have time to get through the previous questions. Ask staff members to share what things should be stopped because they were not effective or caused harm. Next, have them share any ideas they feel are worthy of starting in the school and anything they feel is important to continue doing. After meeting individually with staff, compile their stop, start, and continue ideas into a chart and share it with them when it is time to move forward.

If you have a parent council or parent-teacher association, it is a good idea to schedule a meet and greet with them before the year begins. Once again, share your vision and ideas for your school and the year ahead. Be prepared to listen to parent council members' ideas; if an idea makes sense, and you and your staff have the capability, offer suggestions about how you can work together to make the school the best it can be.

Each summer before the school year kicks off, Sheldon Oshio—principal of Waikele Elementary School in Waikele, Hawaii—opens his house up for the annual Ohana Family Picnic. All staff members are invited to bring their families, which helps them get to know each other on a more personal level. According to Oshio, "Seeing and meeting each other's families helps us all feel like one big family. Over the years, we've seen each other's kids grow up" (personal communication, January 8, 2025). For Waikele, the family picnic has been going on for over fifteen years.

Be Visible

It's difficult to build or maintain a relationship with someone you don't see very often. One of the most critical things you can do is to be visible. Visibility can come in many forms, especially at the beginning and end of the school day, as well as during lunch and recess. When staff members see you sharing traffic duty, they will truly feel like you are in it with them, which builds trust. Trust (especially trust built over time) is one of the most important components of a strong relationship (Hitt & Tucker, 2016). Recess and lunch supervisors know you understand the work they do when they see you interacting with students on the playground or at the lunch tables. Those actions can help build relationships.

Visibility also includes making yourself visible in classrooms. For a teacher—especially a newer teacher—having the principal come into their classroom while they're instructing can be an intimidating experience. It makes them feel nervous and vulnerable. At the same time, it is an incredible opportunity for you to see them in action and get to know the real work happening in their classroom. Once teachers and students see you in their classroom a few times, they'll get used to it and will appreciate your visibility.

At the end of her classroom visits, former principal-turned-superintendent Nichole Burgin always made sure to leave a sticky note with something positive written on it for the teacher. The teachers came to really cherish these notes, and many began posting them on their boards for everyone to see (N. Burgin, personal communication, January 10, 2025). With a small note, Burgin was building relationships with her teachers by being visible. She showed teachers that she was paying attention to what was happening in their classrooms.

Include Teachers in the Planning (Especially Experienced Ones)

Just as everyone on your staff wants to feel seen, they also want to feel included, especially veteran teachers who have valuable insight built by devoting years to your school and community. Whenever possible, involving faculty and staff in decisions that affect them helps greatly with that inclusiveness. In many cases, you might not reach a point where everyone agrees—get used to that—but you can work to make sure everyone feels heard in the decision-making process.

What's the best way to make sure everyone feels heard? Just ask them how they feel about the topic. Ask everyone during a meeting or ask them individually in passing or in private. You don't need to agree or disagree with them; thank them for their opinion and let them know you value their perspective. Of course, at some point you will need to make a decision. When communicating that decision, acknowledge that you spoke with several people about it and thank them for sharing their thoughts. Even if the decision doesn't go their way, they will likely feel validated and that you were doing more than just listening for listening's sake.

For most principals, veteran teachers are key to this strategy. If you are younger or newer to the profession, veteran teachers who've been at your school site for many years may have outspoken opinions that can feel intimidating, confusing, or frustrating. There can be many reasons for this. They may feel disrespected by the last person in your position, or they may have been working toward something for a long time with limited results. Listening and not discounting the little things are important behaviors for building relationships with those veterans—and perhaps you might even turn an outspoken critic into one of your biggest sources of support.

Listen to Experienced Teachers

Veteran teachers need to feel seen and heard, especially as a new principal enters the school. Their institutional memory and experience at that school make them extremely valuable to everyone. In fact, "school leaders that allow veteran teachers to engage in the decision making processes related to curriculum issues, staff development, and student discipline as well as other areas of concern are more likely to retain experienced educators" (Durham, Norton, Bird, & Ohlson, 2017, p. 85). They've put in many years at this school and have possibly seen many principals (with many different styles of leadership) come and go. Value their institutional knowledge and ask lots of questions about their experiences. After they tell you their thoughts and experiences, be sure to let them know how it has informed your thinking and leadership decisions. Such questions might include the following.

- What are some of the biggest changes you've seen at this school in the years you've been here?
- What were some defining characteristics of the best principal you worked with? (If you really want to go for it, follow this question up with, How can I be even better than they were?)
- In your experience, what systems were in place when this school was at its best?
- What is one thing I can take off your plate to make your job easier, if possible?

Don't Discount the Little Things From Experienced Teachers

Especially for some veteran teachers who have decades of experience with other administrators, small things can become very important. Perhaps they've been asking for a light to be fixed for weeks, months, or (hopefully not) years now. That light might not be high on your list of importance, but it's been a source of great frustration for them—and perhaps even symbolic of how they feel they are treated by administrators in general. Imagine how much more open they'll be to participating in the professional development you offer later if they feel heard in these smaller ways.

Find out what's important to your faculty and staff, respect it, and show them it's important to you as well, whenever possible. (Now, how quickly can you help get that light fixed?)

Know the Contract

It might not be the most interesting piece of advice on this list, but knowing the teacher's contract—and exactly what is and isn't expected of them—can be a lifesaver on occasion. For example, throughout the year, your staff will come to you needing time off for a variety of reasons. While their reasons might be valid and important, you obviously won't be able to grant all requests. You do not want to base decisions on instinct or make them without specific criteria—or worse, be accused of basing decisions on who you like. Thus, referring all requests to the contractual agreement will save you time (along with potential favoritism) and make it clear why you made those decisions.

Consider table 2.2 to understand the nuances of teacher and principal relationships.

Table 2.2: Shifting Relationships

As a Teacher	As a Principal
You build new relationships with students and their families each year. At the end of the school year, they move on to another teacher or school.	You are building relationships with teachers and staff members who will return each year, often over several years.
For students, it's totally normal to have a new teacher each year.	For teachers, it can be disheartening to have a new principal each year.
You probably don't have much interaction with your district superintendent.	You will communicate with your district superintendent on a regular basis.

Start With the Interview

Keep in mind that building relationships with your teachers begins well before they start teaching. As the principal, you'll have the opportunity to meet many of your teachers when they first come in to interview for the job. Just as it is an opportunity for them to make a great impression on you, remember that you are also making an impression on them. While *you* are asking them about their experience and expertise, *they* are asking themselves, "Is this someone I really want to work for?"

Attracting and retaining effective teachers who contribute positively to your school community can be tough. You can minimize turnover by hiring the right people the first time around. According to Paul G. Young (2023), past president of the National Association of Elementary School Principals:

> Ultimately, an interview at our school became a conversation about finding, accepting, and nurturing individuals who wanted to join a professional staff where work was valued, appreciated, and rewarded. We were determined to find people who would make our team better and would want to stick around. If candidates didn't already have a pattern of work habits that aligned with that vision, they often chose to go elsewhere.

Build Relationships With Students

As principal, the seemingly endless lists of duties, responsibilities, and urgent matters can often take you away from the reason you got into this work in the first place—*the students*. As you grapple with decisions about budgets, personnel, curricula, and other topics in (and outside) your role as the school's leader, remember that cultivating relationships with the students you serve will help you keep your work in perspective. It will also help keep you inspired to continue with this work each day. Plus, building relationships with students is super fun! You may not see the exact same students each day like you did when you were a classroom teacher, but you are going to see many *more* students and have opportunities to build relationships with them in all sorts of different ways.

Here are some ways you can build relationships with students each day.

- Learn names.
- Show up.
- Remember what it means to get sent to the principal's office.
- Be visible.

Learn Names

While students expect their teachers will learn their names, they often come to expect that the principal won't. Getting to know your students' names (at least as many as possible) shows that you see them and that they are important to you. It's not easy, but you can do it. To expedite this memorization, consider looking through last year's yearbook to match photos with names (and watch students' faces light up when you use their names upon meeting them) or current photos that are posted in classrooms or around the school. Taking the time to learn their names shows students that they matter (Merrigan, 2024).

Susanna Ramirez, principal of Robert C. Cooley Middle School in Roseville, California, introduces herself to students as often as possible and tells them that she wants to remember their names. She then says, "Challenge me to remember your name," and invites them to test her on it, whenever possible (S. Ramirez, personal communication, January 8, 2025). Not only does this accelerate her memorization of students' names, but it also gives students a reason to come up and say hello. (What student doesn't love issuing a name challenge to their principal?) If she can't remember their name when asked, she follows it up with, "Give me a way to remember your name." Students often tell her something about themselves, which helps her build on the relationship even further (S. Ramirez, personal communication, January 8, 2025). The *interactions* are more important than whether she actually knows the student's name, but eventually, she gets those names memorized.

Show Up

Some students shine in the classroom, some shine on the sports field, and others shine on stage or in the art studio. Showing up to extracurricular school and community events that your students are participating in can go a long way in building powerful relationships with them (and their families, which will be discussed next). Plus, you'll have something to talk with them about when you see them on campus the next day.

You might keep the following in mind so you can show up without it taking too much of your time.

- **Go where the numbers are:** It might sound obvious, but showing up to events that involve more students—such as sporting events and music or theater performances—allows you to show many students (and their families) that you are interested in their lives outside the traditional daytime setting.
- **Go beyond the obvious:** There are, of course, students who don't participate in the more mainstream activities. Keep an eye and ear out for the less obvious opportunities, like the poetry slam at the local bookstore or the cultural event happening over the weekend. For many students, their true passions exist in what they do outside of school, and your presence can go a long way toward building powerful, positive relationships.
- **Batch them:** You can save yourself time and energy by grouping similar events when possible and trying to attend them in one block of time. Instead of attending a play on Wednesday, a dance performance on Thursday, and a football game on Friday, look for opportunities where a few (or several) events are happening on the same day. Then, drop in to some or all of them during a specified amount of time. Your students and their families will appreciate seeing you there, and saying "I really need to get to the next event" will give you a good reason to keep moving!

Remember What It Means to Get Sent to the Principal's Office

Getting sent to the principal's office usually only means one thing: You're in trouble! When a student shows up at your office, they're usually bringing with them a mixed bag of emotions, including anger, embarrassment, frustration, or sadness.

As the principal, you often make the final decision regarding what will happen with this student. Listen with an open heart, but don't be afraid to make decisions that are in the best interest of everyone involved. If a student needs to receive a consequence for their actions, deliver it with confidence and clarity. Having clear, well-defined policies in place will help you follow through while minimizing confusion or disparities. Once you make your decision, communicate clearly with the student, their parents or guardians, and the teachers involved. Even if someone doesn't agree with your decision, clear and open communication will help build the relationship. Make sure that communication clearly states the who, what, when, where, and why of the situation. Keep a written record of your conversation if you deliver the news via phone call.

Be Visible

Yes, it's a theme! Like building relationships with teachers and staff, being visible on the playground, in the hallways, in classrooms, during lunch, and before and after school is critical to building relationships with students. When students see you, they'll feel like they are getting to know you (and you are getting to know them).

Of course, whenever you see students, be sure to say, "Hi!" or better yet, "Hi, (*first name*)!" Do you want to really mix things up? Head into the cafeteria at lunch one day and help serve the food, throw on your tennis shoes and head outside to join a physical education class (especially when you might need an office break), or jump into the band practice and show them what you've got.

Build Relationships With Parents and Guardians

Families send their children to school each day with the hope that they will return smarter, more confident, and more aware of the world around them. While families send their children to us with deep care for their future, they also worry about their safety and emotional well-being—sometimes, they just hope their child will make it through the day. While most families are well aware of who their child's teacher is, they might not necessarily know much about the principal—especially if you're new.

Of course, no two families are the same. The families of some students who have been a part of your school community for many years never come to school. Others will be at your office door every week to express an opinion or question a decision. It's important to build relationships with *all* families. Regardless of the level of involvement, capitalize on an asset-based approach, which recognizes that families have strengths, skills, and resources that support their students and their learning (Wells, 2023).

The following are some ways you can proactively build relationships with parents and guardians, ensuring that they feel their children are in good hands and that the right person is leading their school.

- Plan meet and greets.
- Make positive phone calls home.
- Communicate using email newsletters, text, and phone services.
- Be visible.

Plan Meet and Greets

Planning a short event where families can meet you is a great way to quickly increase your visibility and meet several parents and guardians in a specified time frame.

The beginning of the school year (especially a few days before the students return to school) is a great time to plan this. A simple, hour-long Come Meet the New Principal event starting at 3:00 p.m. in the cafeteria is all you need to kick things off. Do you really want to make sure people come visit? You can entice them with something fun like a taco truck or a snow cone maker.

Of course, many parents and guardians will have to work during these events, so consider doing something at a nontraditional time. Similar to the taco truck idea, maybe you'll have a dessert offering later in the evening.

Have a translator there to help families who do not speak English (if you don't speak their native language), *and* let everyone know in advance that the translator will be there. This establishes trust and helps you build relationships with everyone, not just the highly visible. You might need translators for multiple different languages. If you're not sure where to get that information, start with your school's attendance clerk (or the person who sits at the front desk in the office where families enter the school).

It doesn't have to be at the beginning of the school year—families will appreciate the chance to meet you at any time throughout the year. Leticia Arroyo, principal of Mission Middle School in Escondido, California, held a monthly, hour-long Coffee With the Principal event where families could come in, ask questions, discuss their concerns, and—as the name suggests—just have a cup of coffee.

Make Positive Phone Calls Home

Imagine being a parent and receiving a call from your child's principal to tell you about something *great* your child did! Not only would you feel good, but you would also be much more likely to pick up the phone the next time their principal called.

It's important to reach out to parents and guardians for a multitude of reasons. Because some of those reasons aren't good news, it's more important to reach out with positive connection and acknowledgment, too. When you have already started building a relationship with a parent or guardian before giving them bad news, your conversation can be focused on solutions. Even if you haven't already interacted with the person you are calling, they are likely to be more receptive to the negative call if they have seen you in front of the school during morning drop-off or if you've waved goodbye to them at the end of the day.

Susanna Ramirez, the principal that has students challenge her to remember their names, utilizes what she calls positive principal calls. She simply asks teachers and staff to write something positive that one of their students has done—a nice way to start a staff meeting—and she calls home to let the parent or guardian know about it. Each call takes just a minute or two, and she sets aside a short block of time to make several phone calls. According to Ramirez, "A phone call is always better than a text or email. Even if you leave a message, the parent really appreciates hearing your voice" (personal communication, January 8, 2025). You can visit www.instagram.com/mrglynnprincipal/reel/DCl53kIx6d8 to watch Michael Glynn, the principal at Central Community

Elementary in Newport, Maine, make a positive phone call home to a parent. Notice how much the parent appreciates it.

It may be tougher to find something positive to share about some students. Again, keep an asset-based approach and be creative with what you can celebrate. Did they have two weeks of perfect attendance, an improvement on their latest test score, or something as simple as crossing the street safely? For those parents and guardians, the fact that you called to share something positive will far outweigh the specifics of your call.

Make sure the communication works both ways—when a parent or guardian says something nice about their child's teacher, be sure to let that teacher know. Hearing it from you gives that teacher a heightened sense of pride, it helps you build a strong relationship with that teacher, and it connects the teacher with the family.

Tips to Thrive

The following are three ways to start a conversation with a parent or guardian when you need to make a phone call home about something that isn't positive.

1. "Hi, this is Mr. Tuckey, the principal at McIntire Elementary. I'm calling regarding something that happened at school today, and since you know Eddie better than anyone, I'd really like to talk to you about it."
2. "Hi, Mr. Smith, this is principal Tuckey. The last time we spoke, I told you about when Megan helped a new student. This time around, I'm calling for a different reason."
3. "Hi, Ms. Muñoz. We need to talk." (This option obviously doesn't start out as friendly as the first two but helps convey the seriousness of the conversation you're about to have. As the principal, you'll decide the tone and seriousness that you want the conversation to have.)

Communicate Using Email Newsletters, Text, and Phone Services

Services such as ParentSquare (www.parentsquare.com) allow you to send out a text or prerecorded phone call to all your families and staff members. While you might not use these services to build one-to-one relationships, they provide an opportunity for you to quickly connect with many people. Whether you send it out once weekly or monthly, consistency is key, and success is based on "consistency in delivery, clarity of articles, and timeliness of content" (Schneider & Hollenczer, 2006, p. 147). You should know what you are communicating in advance. Is it school news or upcoming events and holidays, or are you inviting parents and guardians to respond with thoughts and feedback?

The tone you set through your communications is important. While it might seem like a simple snow-day announcement to some, adding something funny or inspirational will help families get to know you in small ways. Although it's a one-way communication and doesn't necessarily build a relationship, it can help increase your approachability. And the more people feel you are approachable, the more these relationships will benefit over time.

Be Visible

We have already mentioned how critically important it is for teachers, staff, and students to see you as often as possible—the same goes for parents and guardians. Even if you can't interact with each of them before and after school, they will appreciate seeing you interact with others.

Nichole Burgin has a simple strategy that she utilizes. In the morning, she prioritizes greeting students as they walk onto campus, and then she prioritizes chatting with families in the afternoon. Of course, she ends up building relationships with both groups. She also makes it a point to greet someone she hasn't met yet. All it takes is one interaction with a parent or guardian, and you're on your way to building a personal relationship with them (N. Burgin, personal communication, January 8, 2025).

Tips to Thrive

Don't forget that building marquee! Families and other community members pass your school's marquee daily, which means every day is an opportunity to interact with them. While you probably can't change the message daily—even though digital marquees do make it pretty easy—posting good news or asking a fun question gives you the opportunity to communicate with and convey explicit and implicit messages to anyone passing by. While you are not building a relationship with passersby, you are helping build and convey the school culture, and relationships thrive in a positive culture.

Build Relationships With District-Level Administrators

As a teacher, you may have had some interaction with your district's superintendent or other district leaders (such as assistant superintendents or program directors). It was probably limited compared to the interactions you'll have with them as a principal. Keep in mind that every district is different in why, how often, and to what extent the superintendent interacts with principals.

While it is the superintendent's job to build relationships with their principals (just as you proactively build relationships with your teachers), the following list offers ways you can build relationships with your superintendent and other district leaders.

- Know the hierarchy and chain of command.
- Invite them in.
- Ask questions.
- Be honest.

Know the Hierarchy and Chain of Command

Some superintendents want you to communicate directly with their assistant superintendents, while others want you to come directly to them. (In many cases, the bigger the district, the more people there are between you and the superintendent.) As in many schools, there's often the *official* communication flowchart, and then there's the *unofficial* (here's how the culture really is here) flowchart around how people communicate. You're learning the hidden curricula—the norms, values, and beliefs that aren't explicitly taught but are understood—just like everyone does in a new space (Chatelain, 2018).

Pay attention and become familiar with both hierarchies and expectations, and then use your best judgment when deciding how to best communicate with your leadership. Other principals and district leaders' assistants can be good sources of information about how to successfully navigate the hierarchy.

Invite Them In

You needn't wait for someone to tell you they're visiting campus. If there's something happening that you're excited about, be proactive and invite them. Special events or celebrations are great reasons to reach out and invite them in, especially if there's going to be media there covering the event. However, these events are not the only reasons to invite them.

Has your staff been incorporating a new teaching strategy they're excited about? Invite your superintendent or others to see it happening in person. Were you planning to read one of your favorite children's books to a class on Friday? Invite them to read one of their favorite books to a class, too.

Most district leaders were once teachers themselves. They may love an opportunity to connect with students. When they do, you can build your relationship with them at the same time.

Ask Questions

One of the most effective ways to build relationships and get clarity around your work is to simply ask questions. The following questions not only help you grow your relationship with your district-level administrators but also help you be more effective in the work you do each day.

- What and when are the best ways to communicate with you?
- How do you describe your management style?

- Who do you lean on the most in your role?
- What can I do, as principal, to best support you?
- How would you describe the school culture up to this point?

You can ask these questions while you are interviewing for the job, during a meeting (perhaps before the school year), or in an email. Regardless of how you ask, keep in mind that, someday in the future, a new principal might be asking you these questions.

Be Honest

It can be intimidating to discuss with your superintendent the struggles and challenges you're facing as the school's leader. For example, it can be tempting to only walk your district leaders through classrooms with strong teachers where things are often going well. However, it is a good idea to walk them through the classrooms where you know a teacher might be struggling as well.

Don't be afraid to discuss this with them, though. Remember, part of their job is to help support you and to help you and your school be successful. Most superintendents and district leaders were once in your shoes as principals. They may even have been at the same school you're at now.

Keep these strategies in mind when you need to reach out for help.

- **Start lightly:** Just like when calling a parent or guardian at home, open with something positive or funny before moving onto the problem. This shows that you have things in perspective and aren't calling only for the negative things.
- **Be proactive:** When you see something occurring that families may need to hear about, let the superintendent know *before* the parent or teacher reaches out to them. This can help them avoid feeling blindsided by an issue.
- **Be appropriately transparent when possible:** Trust builds transparency and vice versa. When you're appropriately transparent and open about challenges, it often results in a culture of trust (Ratanjee, 2022).

As mentioned earlier, it isn't unlikely that you will one day be in the role of program director, assistant superintendent, or superintendent. Pay attention to how the people in these roles are building relationships with you and incorporate and adapt any helpful strategies into your own leadership (now and in the future).

Build Relationships With Your Site Leadership Team

According to early explorer Ernest Shackleton, "Leadership is a fine thing, but it has its penalties. And the greatest penalty is loneliness" (as cited in Morrell & Capparell, 2001, p. 215). Even though you're surrounded by hundreds or thousands of students and their families, teachers, and staff, all day long, leadership can be a lonely gig. There will be times when it seems like every decision, every course correction, and every complaint falls right onto your shoulders. But you are not alone, and one of the best things you can do to ensure your success is surround yourself with a leadership team of people you trust who bring out the best in each other.

There are, of course, the obvious members of your leadership team: your assistant principal, dean of students, school secretary, and front office manager. Consider adding to your team any less obvious people who have a big impact on your school and who can help support you in a multitude of ways. These people might include the following.

- Head custodian
- Teacher leaders (such as your department chairs or grade-level leads)
- Coaches
- Attendance clerk
- Food service leaders
- Parents, grandparents, and guardians
- Students

Wondering about the best way to approach these people to be a part of the team? Ask them in person. Asking for a favor in person yields far greater results than sending an email, texting, or calling (Roghanizad & Bohns, 2021). Keep this in mind any time you need to lead someone to say "yes!"

Once you've got your team in place, here are simple ways to build and strengthen your relationships with them.

- Empower them to make decisions.
- Get targeted training for them.
- Say "thank you."

Empower Them to Make Decisions

Empowering your site team to make decisions (and then trusting them enough to get out of their way) is a powerful way to build relationships with them (Leithwood, Harris, & Hopkins, 2020). You increase the leadership capacity across your school at the same time.

In *Fierce Conversations: Achieving Success at Work and in Life One Conversation at a Time*, Susan Scott (2002) encourages leaders to work with their teams to use the Decision Tree model. This model helps determine what decisions and actions employees can take with and without needing to get their leader's approval. Scott (2002) discusses four types of decisions; each level is based on a part of a tree, ranging from least to most critical for the tree to flourish.

1. **Leaf decisions:** An employee makes a decision, acts on it, and does not need to report back to the boss on the action taken. Examples of leaf decisions follow.

- The English department chair meets with the leadership group, and they decide to switch the order in which they will teach some of the upcoming content.
- A parent or guardian comes into the front office to speak to the teacher about their child's behavior, and the front desk clerk connects them with the school counselor instead.

2. **Branch decisions:** An employee makes a decision, acts on it, then later reports on it to their boss. Examples of branch decisions follow.
    - An assistant principal determines a student's disciplinary action and copies you on the email to their parent, letting them know what consequences their child faces.
    - Your head custodian closes a part of campus to make a repair. They need to let you know that it will be closed until it is fixed, but they don't need to ask you for permission to close it.
3. **Trunk decisions:** An employee makes a decision and reports on it before taking any action. Examples of trunk decisions follow.
    - The teachers in your mathematics department decide to use a new program to supplement their teaching. Before they start using it, they reach out to you to see if you have any additional thoughts on how they can use it.
    - The cafeteria staff want to change some of the items that they serve at lunch. They know that there might be some additional costs associated with this decision, so they check with you first to make sure it is within the budget.
4. **Root decisions:** An employee goes directly to their boss before making any decisions and includes them in the steps moving forward. Examples of root decisions include the following.
    - You must address any safety issues that need immediate attention, from major damage to an intruder.
    - You can change the time or location of a special event due to unexpected need.

As you can see, the decisions range in autonomy, which build trust and strengthen your relationships. When your team knows that you trust them to make decisions, they can make them with confidence, and it frees you up to do the work you need to do.

Keep in mind that mistakes are going to happen. Approach mistakes with compassion and understanding, and take the steps necessary to avoid them in the future.

Get Targeted Training for Them

Recognizing that your leadership team is filled with actual leaders means there are certain skills and strategies they need to effectively do their jobs. Find out what they feel they need or are struggling with and get them training in that specific area.

Is one of your assistant principals struggling to coach teachers? Look into some professional development for them specifically on coaching (chances are, they won't be the only one who needs this). Does your front office manager need a bit of extra support while learning the new computer or data system the district just implemented? Perhaps there's someone from your information technology department who can help.

Of course, some might disagree with you about the training you believe they need. When that happens, have an open conversation with them about it, and, when necessary, bring in any data that might help you make the case for what you believe they need to learn more about. The bottom line is that the more effectively and confidently your leadership team does their jobs, the better and stronger your relationship with them will be and the more time you'll have for your own work (like getting out to that pickup line after school).

Say "Thank You"

As simple as it might seem, everyone—at every level—likes to be appreciated for the work they do. Finding ways to say "thank you" to your leadership team will help them feel appreciated, seen, and valued. Sheldon Oshio, the principal mentioned earlier, knows how important his office staff are and always orders a birthday cake whenever it is an office staff member's special day. With each slice, Sheldon's staff members know they are valued and that relationships are at the center of every bite.

Research supports expressing gratitude to others, showing that it "has a positive impact on motivation, happiness and contentment" (Patil, Biswas, & Kaur, 2019, p. 21). It is more impactful to not go overboard by thanking people too often and to express your appreciation to a specific person versus thanking a group of people in general (Patil et al., 2019). This expressed appreciation to teachers actually impacts students in that "appreciation of teachers and teachers' competence have a positive and significant correlation" (Yoestara, Putri, & Ismail, 2020, p. 47).

Build Relationships With the Wider Community

Every shop owner in your city knows how critical it is to build relationships with their local community, and every knowledgeable CEO understands the impact their company has on the surrounding area. The school you lead often holds both sentimental value and cultural significance in the surrounding area. Many people in the community attended the school, and many are employed in the school or district. And the students who attend your school are often some of the most visible community members. In short, your school is inextricably linked to the community, and as the principal, so are you. Building relationships with the wider community plays an important role in the success of your school and the entire community.

Here are some ways you can proactively connect with the wider community and help minimize or eliminate potential conflicts.

- Get to know business owners in your school's neighborhood.
- Invite local businesspeople and leaders to come to school

Get to Know Business Owners in Your School's Neighborhood

If it's possible in your school's neighborhood, walk around and visit the local businesses. Get a coffee, drop off your dry cleaning, or get a haircut. As you get out into the community and get to know folks, they will know you and feel connected to your school. It's also a good idea to get to know the people who run your local library and other nonprofit services that support your school's community.

When school dismisses at Susanna Ramirez's middle school, many of the students head down to the local grocery store to grab a snack and hang out. This doesn't always sit well with the customers or the grocery store manager. When the store manager calls the school, they know to ask for Ramirez directly and can handle things calmly, because the relationship is in place. Ramirez also takes the time to speak to students about being respectful when out in public and how they are a reflection of the school; she even heads down to the grocery store some days so she can be visible to the students and store employees (S. Ramirez, personal communication, January 8, 2025). Once again, visibility is critical!

After building a relationship with the manager of the local hardware store, Sheldon Oshio guided some of the students at his school to reach out to the manager about the store donating some much-needed supplies for the school's gardening club. Not only did they get the supplies they needed, but the hardware store also took an interest in their gardening club. The students are building their own relationships with the wider community. According to Oshio, "When students understand that they represent the school when they are out in the community, the community understands what a great place our school is" (personal communication, January 8, 2025).

Invite Local Businesspeople and Leaders to Come to School

Just as it's important to get ourselves and our students out into the community, inviting the community to come into the school also helps build relationships. Whether it's for events like career day or to speak to an individual class, inviting local business owners, city government workers or representatives, or others from the community can make these individuals feel important and connected—and that they have a stake in your school's success.

In Maine, many of the banks have employee programs that require them to volunteer in the community. According to Holly Blair, executive director of Maine Principals' Association:

> A lot of the employees want to volunteer, but they don't know where to go. We invite them into our schools to help out and talk to our students about financial literacy. It's a great partnership, and a lot of great relationships are built. The bottom line is schools can't work in isolation. (personal communication, January 8, 2025)

Final Thoughts: Relationships Are Full Circle

When building relationships, it's important to remember the difference between relationships and friendships. While all of your friendships require you to be in a relationship, not every relationship requires you to be friends. As with all the examples in this chapter, it is critical to keep in mind that the relationships you are building need to stay in a professional and public capacity.

A school leader can find themselves in a tough situation when a relationship moves from professional to personal, so make sure to keep your relationships professional. Not only will this help you stay clear in your vision and mission (as outlined in the previous chapter), but it will also help you avoid your colleagues feeling like you might favor one over another or have favorites at all.

However you decide to build relationships with your colleagues, students, their families, and the community, remember that today's community members were yesterday's students. And today's students are tomorrow's employees, neighbors, and hopefully even teachers (and principals)!

Now that you're a principal, each day is an opportunity to show your school and neighborhood that relationships are at the heart of the critical work you do. From simply saying hello to empowering those around you to make confident decisions, when you build relationships as a school principal, you're building them for an entire community.

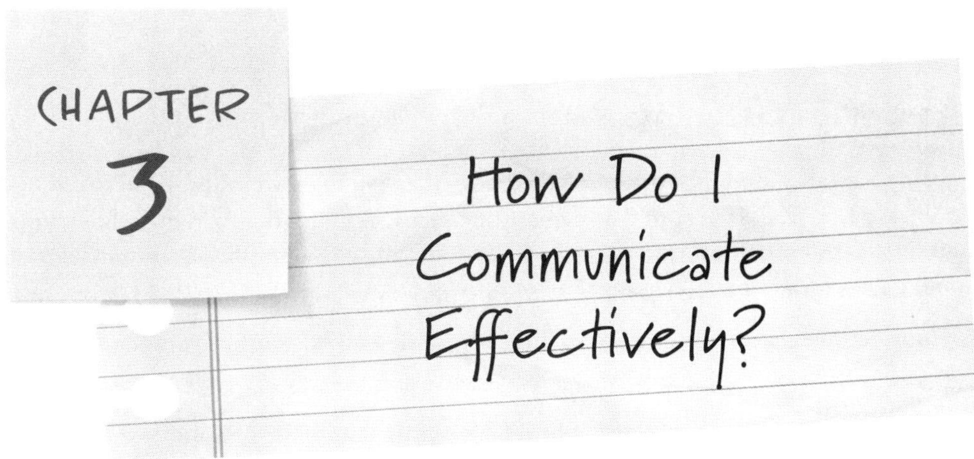

Chapter 3: How Do I Communicate Effectively?

Effective communication is key to your success as a principal, and recognizing that communication isn't just verbal is important. Your body language, listening skills, actions, moods, and behaviors must align with what you say. It is so important for you to share your vision for student learning and what you want for your school. Your staff, students, families, and broader community need to know what you stand for. Research proves this point and makes evident how clear communication is directly tied to positive relationships:

> Successful principals communicate purposefully, implementing strategies like "open door" policies, sending weekly emails with information staff need and recognition of staff contributions, and being willing to have challenging conversations with staff when necessary. Effective communication can build shared expectations, which predicts teacher satisfaction, cohesion, and commitment to the school. (Grissom et al., 2021, p. 56)

The good news is that you have ample opportunities to share your message when leading meetings, writing emails and newsletters, and having pertinent conversations. As a principal, you cannot overcommunicate as you seek to create your own narrative. In the absence of that narrative, there are those who will fill the gap with misinformation or negativity. Ask yourself, "Is the story being told about my school the one my team and I know to be true?" If your answer is "yes," this chapter provides suggestions to deepen your work in communication. If your answer is "no," the suggestions and ideas that follow will help you build a foundation to improve your school's narrative.

Communicating effectively starts with listening, modeling your vision, setting boundaries, leading effective meetings, engaging staff, writing effective messaging, and preparing for tough conversations.

Start With Listening

Being a good communicator doesn't just mean that you share your ideas; you also must be a good listener. Make sure that when someone is speaking that you give them your undivided attention and truly listen to what they have to say. Active listening helps us build relationships, resolve conflicts, and truly hear a message (Farmer, 2025).

Consider these possible actions that can aid you in active listening.

- Sit across from or beside them.
- Take notes if that is helpful; offer them a copy or a follow-up phone call or email.
- Make appropriate eye contact.
- Put away your phone and, if necessary, move to a quiet space.
- Paraphrase what they've said.
- Seek clarity about anything that is unclear.

Model Your Vision

Communicating isn't just saying or writing words. Modeling is also a form of communication. Therefore, it is imperative that you live your vision. This helps prevent perceived contradictions between what you say and what you do—this mixed messaging is also a communication but not a positive one. If your vision is "Ensuring all students reach their academic potential," then you must create the environment and the sense of urgency in your staff to make this vision a reality. If when meeting with a caregiver, you tell them that you are looking for solutions to support their child while you simultaneously look at the clock, your actions do not align with your words. Work collaboratively with parents and guardians to find solutions for their concerns and follow up after to confirm that the solution has resolved the issue. This builds trust with both the caregiver and the child.

Consistency in what you say and how you act will be noticed by all stakeholders. If you don't have a vision, use it as your guide, and model the behaviors aligned with it, you will not be working toward improvement for student learning. If you share a vision of academic success, but then you accept that 20 percent of students are failing a course, your actions don't align with your vision. These inconsistencies derail the work. One of Tom's favorite quotes is "If you condone it, you own it!" Remember that how you speak, your decisions, and your actions all must be aligned and shared through modeling.

Educator and author Baruti K. Kafele also believes in the importance of modeling your vision. Kafele (2024) uses a daily self-reflective process to confirm he is modeling his vision and recommends asking yourself these questions every day:

Is my school a better place because I lead it?

What is my value to the staff and students I serve?

Does instruction in my school thrive under my leadership?

Is there a correlation between my leadership and student academic outcomes?

What is the overall experience of being a student, teacher, and leader in my school?

Set Boundaries

While it is imperative that you are visible and available for your students, staff, and families, it is also important that you set boundaries around your time. While instructional leadership is ultimately your greatest responsibility, you have many other responsibilities that take time away from that important work. Email, while a wonderful invention, can eat up many hours of your time. Set aside thirty minutes—either first thing in the morning or at the end of the day—and make that a sacred time to address your email. If you cannot immediately answer someone's request, let them know that you've read their email and will get back to them as soon as you can investigate the situation. (You don't want stakeholders to think you're ignoring them.) Then, follow up in no longer than forty-eight hours.

You will often feel pulled in several directions; lots of people will want time with you. Your administrative assistant, who can act as a gatekeeper for the times you are available, is one of your greatest allies. Many administrators also communicate their availability in their out-of-office voice message—for example, "I am out in classrooms supporting teachers and students and will return your call when I am back in my office." Sharing or displaying a schedule of your office times can also help communicate your availability.

Set boundaries for your communication in addition to allotting email time. One strategy is to set a six-to-six protocol, which means that you are available to receive and respond to email and phone messages between 6 a.m. and 6 p.m. Make sure staff know to text or call you in case of an emergency outside of those hours. It is also critical that you set and live by those boundaries with your staff. Model this expectation as well; don't infringe on your staff's personal time.

Lead Effective Meetings

Leading effective meetings is another way you can respect your time and others'. In this section, we look at the first staff meeting of the year and regular meetings. Your first staff meeting—the first formal time you are with your staff—sets the tone for the year. Regular staff meetings allow you to home in on priorities.

First Staff Meeting of the Year

Your first staff meeting of the year should be used to convey your vision and outline procedures and practices that are important for ensuring a safe and caring learning environment. Prior to this meeting, you should meet with staff individually to check in and see where they are at and how you can support them moving forward.

A first staff meeting agenda could include items such as the following.

- Create norms for working together as a team.
- Introduce yourself and your vision for the school.
- Share any district and school policies that may be new or updated.

Norms are a set of rules that outline how staff members interact with one another. Norms help establish clear expectations for behavior, communication, and collaboration among team members. Creating norms for collaborating during meetings is important groundwork. They can be guidelines for working and interacting with others or expectations for getting the work done.

You can establish norms via team discussions, onboarding processes, and team-building activities. It's important for all team members to have a voice in this process to ensure buy-in and commitment. Everyone in the group contributes to a list of what behaviors they would like to see during meetings and discussions. Once ideas have been collected, the group narrows them down to five or so statements that become the framework for working collaboratively. Typically, norms include topics like the following.

- **Respectful communication:** Listening actively and valuing diverse opinions
- **Accountability:** Taking responsibility for individual tasks and commitments
- **Collaboration:** Encouraging teamwork and supporting others in achieving shared goals
- **Feedback culture:** Giving and receiving constructive feedback regularly to promote growth

As a group, you collectively agree on the behaviors that will work best for all involved to get the work done in an effective and respectful manner. Regularly revisiting and adjusting norms may be necessary as the team evolves or faces new challenges.

One school we worked with collaboratively created the following set of norms that they use at the start of every meeting (M. Crozier, personal communication, 2024).

- Be tough on the issues, not on the people.
- Everyone's voice should be heard.
- Discussions need to be student centered.
- Come prepared for the meeting.

As you can see, norms are usually developed to outline respectful behavior—very similar to classroom rules.

One school uses the phrase "Here we ROAR" as their mantra, which stands for *respect*, *ownership*, *achievement*, and *responsibility* (École Sifton School, n.d.). Another school had the "Cougar Code: Achieving Success Together," which highlights three key areas of respect with indicators of what each behavior looked like and sounded like (École Charlie Killam School, n.d.):

1. Respect Yourself—be prepared for learning; use time effectively
2. Respect Others—respect everyone's right to learn; demonstrate good sportsmanship
3. Respect Our School—keep areas tidy around your locker and desk; recycle, reduce, reuse

Having a set of norms or a mantra that guides how people in your building—including staff, students, and visitors—behave makes it easier to work through meetings or deal with unpleasant situations. You can always refer people back to these norms, mantras, or codes.

Once you've created a set of norms for working with your staff, these can be used in a variety of settings besides staff meetings. They can also be used in professional learning settings. It's a good idea to print the norms and remind everyone of the agreed-on behaviors for working together at the beginning of each session. There may also be occasions where you will want to revise them.

Follow these steps to create norms.

1. Ask your staff members to think about the best team meeting they have ever participated in. Have members call out their responses while you record them on chart paper.
2. Ask them to think about a time when they were involved in a team meeting and things didn't go well. Discuss what would have helped to make things better. Ensure that their responses are added if they weren't already recorded in step 1.
3. Ask your staff members to reflect on this conversation and the ideas you've recorded on the chart paper. Ask them to use this information to determine three to five norms they all agree on that will guide future meetings and group work.
4. Record these norms on chart paper that can be displayed at future meetings and group work sessions. You may want to reproduce them on card stock so they can be laid out on tables going forward.

Leaders play a crucial role in modeling and reinforcing norms. Model the behaviors you wish to see and hold your team members accountable to these standards. Possible norms and examples of each follow.

- **Be tough on the issues, not on the people:** If student behavior is a problem, focus on the behaviors and positive solutions, not on those who were supervising at the time.
- **Listen to everyone's voice:** Everyone should take turns instead of one or two people holding the floor during an entire meeting.
- **Center student discussions:** Some administrators have a parking lot where staff can record items that aren't student centered but need to be followed up on.
- **Come prepared for the meeting:** Be ready in advance and share agendas at least two days prior to the corresponding meeting.

The principal or assistant principal should give gentle reminders if staff stray from the norms. However, sometimes emotions hinder a positive way forward. You may have to stop a specific discussion and set it aside for another meeting. You may also need to address staff members privately to remind them of norms. Leadership is not easy, and this is one area where you need to take the lead.

Regular Staff Meetings

Regularly scheduled staff meetings need to occur. Ensure the following during these meetings.

- Make valuable use of staff time.
- Don't include items that can be shared by email or memo.
- Have meetings last no longer than an hour and a half.
- Start and end on time.
- Precede meetings with an agenda.
- Include interaction so staff know they can provide ideas and be heard.
- If you want staff to have input, share it with them so they are prepared for what you will be discussing.
- Put items in a parking lot to be discussed later if they are causing you to stray from your agenda.

Many principals have a short meeting during the second week of the month and then a longer meeting during the fourth week. The short meeting could last approximately an hour where you check in with staff on a particular goal that you're working on. The second staff meeting of the month should be an hour and a half. People can only endure so much, especially if they've worked all day and then are expected to participate in a staff meeting.

There are always many things to discuss with your staff. Maybe you are having staff try a new instructional strategy in their classes and want to check in to see how it's going. This is an opportunity to hear what is working and what isn't and then decide whether you need to make some changes or stay the course. This shorter meeting is a good opportunity to have some teachers who are having success share what they are doing, which will help others. For example, you might be working on cooperative learning strategies, so you want to hear how many staff members have tried to implement a cooperative learning strategy in their classes and what results they're noticing. Are students more engaged in the lesson? Is attendance improving? If they haven't introduced any of these strategies, this is a good opportunity to have them share what is holding them back.

Creating interactive meetings can be scary if there are some staff who you feel might speak out negatively and derail a good conversation. You can create a seating plan and have staff work in small groups to discuss contentious issues and have one person highlight key discussion ideas the group generates.

Some principals like to start their meetings with staff kudos, where they highlight individual staff members who have gone above and beyond. Maybe they organized a staff lunch or ran a lunch-hour intramural game. This helps build the culture of your school, and your staff should be recognized for their contributions. Other principals like to have staff circulate the room to music. When the music stops, staff members share something about themselves with their closest colleague, like their favorite thing to do or something that makes them happy. This cycle repeats three times just to get staff up and thinking about something positive before they settle in for the meeting. Having snacks at the meeting is advisable.

Once you are more comfortable running meetings, they can have more flexibility. Maybe you have an agenda where various staff members take responsibility for a topic. This allows them the opportunity to lead and take ownership.

The agenda for longer meetings may have standing items such as health and safety, upcoming events, or policy reviews. The rest of the agenda will feature items that are current and either need to be brought to the staff's attention or require their input. Maybe there is a problem such as students vaping in the school. Staff ideas on how to address the problem could be helpful. Be sure they understand that the staff meeting is not a place to call out their colleagues nor is it a complaint session. If a staff member has a concern about a colleague or a situation, that should be addressed individually and professionally. It is also important to ensure that student learning topics (such as literacy rates) form part of this agenda. Again, remember that your vision and purpose need to lead your work.

One sample staff meeting agenda is shown in figure 3.1 (page 42). This is a typical format for an agenda, with some standing items and some that are more specific as issues arise.

Share the agenda electronically with teachers and staff prior to the meeting so they can add items or suggest deletions; something may have been settled since the last meeting, so it doesn't need to be on the agenda for this month. Letting staff see the agenda ahead of time allows them to formulate their ideas prior to the meeting, which allows them to fully participate during the meeting. It's also a good reminder for everyone if you include your vision and purpose statements on the agenda. A visual reminder helps keep people and topics on course.

January 30

Staff Meeting Agenda

1. Additions and deletions
2. Housekeeping and safety
3. School successes
4. School teams—learning consultants and family-school liaisons
5. Technology
6. Athletics
7. Discussion and information items
    - Credit recovery
    - Attendance and late slips
    - Indigenous pathways

Figure 3.1: Example 1 of a staff meeting agenda.

The agenda in figure 3.2 would also be distributed ahead of time so teachers and staff are aware of the items and can add suggestions. This agenda has cooperative learning as an agenda item, which aligns nicely with the school's vision for students to reach their full potential as lifelong learners and its purpose to provide the best possible education by developing a sense of community that values responsibility and curiosity.

November 1

Staff Meeting Agenda

1. Celebrations and successes
2. Pair and share
3. Exams and report cards
4. Enrollment
5. Cooperative learning
6. Individual program plan updates

Figure 3.2: Example 2 of a staff meeting agenda.

Engage Staff

Two-way communication is an effective means of engaging others. Involve staff in important decisions (as discussed with Susan Scott's Decision Tree model in chapter 2, page 15). However, you will have to make some confidential or budgetary decisions. You may still seek staff input but share that you'll make the decision based on the information you've gathered. We find that the more staff are aware of budgetary concerns and big-ticket items that can affect programming, the more likely they are to assume some ownership of the issues. Staff who feel that their voices are heard and respected are far more likely to take a vested interest in being part of the solution. Remember to follow up with your staff following the meeting about what actions have been taken.

Principal H. Zadderey from Grand Trunk High School in Evansburg, Alberta, Canada, adds an exit slip to her staff meeting agenda to identify areas where she can further support her teachers and staff (personal communication, November 5, 2023). You might, for example, ask a simple question such as, "Knowing our goals for the year, what do you need from me to move forward?" Read through the feedback provided. If several people suggest the same idea, group them together and meet with each group. If the ideas are more individualized, you can set aside time to meet with each staff member individually.

Tips to Thrive

Meetings can bring staff together and engage educators in the work, or they can be viewed as a waste of time. If you want a successful meeting, you should be prepared. Have a set agenda, cocreate norms for how staff interact with each other, and start and end the meeting on time.

Write Effective Messaging

Memos, emails, newsletters, daily announcements, handbooks, and online messaging are all important and distinct forms of communication. Remember that "successful principals communicate purposefully" (Grissom et al., 2021, p. 56). These communications are critical to increasing caregiver involvement, which corresponds to higher student achievement, as well as communicating important information to staff and recognizing their hard work (Grissom et al., 2021).

Tips to Thrive

Have a thoughtful outgoing message. In your message, explain briefly that you can't be reached because you are supporting students and teachers in their learning. This emphasizes the importance of teaching and learning.

Memos

Be concise in your messaging, particularly in memos and emails. No one has the time nor the inclination to read three paragraphs when a few sentences will do. Use bullet points, particularly in memos.

Consider sending a weekly memo to staff on Mondays to share key happenings for the week and announce anything new. This is a simple way to ensure that staff are up to date with what's going on in the school that week. It's also helpful for substitute teachers to be aware of anything happening in the school. Figure 3.3 is an example of a memo.

August 12

Monday Morning Memo

"I discovered that a fresh start is a process. A fresh start is a journey—a journey that requires a plan."

—Vivian Jokotade

This week:

- Tuesday—The health nurse is here for grades 6 and 9 students.
- Wednesday—Two substitute teachers are joining us while Sam and Fabi are at professional learning.
- Thursday—The Meet Our Families BBQ is from 4:30 p.m. to 6:30 p.m.
- Friday—The presentation on fire safety is during morning assembly.

Reminders:

- School pictures are next Tuesday.
- Long-range plans are due September 30.
- Professional growth plans are due October 15.
- Please make positive phone calls to families.

Figure 3.3: Example memo.

Emails

Limit the number of emails you send to staff. Often, a quick face-to-face conversation is far more effective and timelier. If you need to send a message, align it with the beginning, middle, or end of the day so staff only need to check once daily for email updates. You may have to send messages for emergent items, but the goal is to avoid requiring staff to check emails when they should be teaching students. Again, be very concise in your communication. Watch for statements that can be negatively construed. Emails can suggest tone and attitude that may not be present.

Email newsletters for families can effectively help you share the information that you want your school community to know.

- Keep the focus on learning and share specific examples from classrooms on a regular basis. It is also a great way to share upcoming events and important dates, but make sure that learning is the key topic.
- Include a section for families about how they can help their child at home. It could include tips about reading with their child or how to access school supports if their child is struggling.
- Be consistent and timely. If you start a newsletter that goes out monthly, make sure that you keep to the schedule. If you send it out sporadically, it will lose its effectiveness as a means of communication.

Tips to Thrive

A school newsletter template is easy to use and provides a professional format. Many newsletter-creating tools are available, and some include a translation option so you can communicate with families whose first language is not English. Balance photos (with parent or guardian permission) and items that relate to learning. Using small sections and bulleted items help to make the newsletter easy to read. You want it to be short enough so that families and the community will read it, but not so long that they won't engage. You can include a student section where students share items about the school or their work (with adult permission). Administrative assistants often take part in writing the newsletter and may compile information from staff and administrators. Some high schools also have students involved in newsletter production. No matter what, it's your job to review that document prior to publication.

Daily Announcements

Daily announcements are a quick and easy way to share items with your students and staff. It's important that staff and students recognize that announcements need to be heard by everyone. You, as the principal, are the best person to share announcements. It's important that everyone in the building knows you support whatever is being announced, and this helps students hear your voice and what you stand for. Alternatively, some schools use announcements as a leadership piece for students. Students from a particular grade (typically grade 6 in an elementary school, grade 9 in a junior high, and grade 12 in a high school) rotate sharing the morning announcements with their peers and the school staff. This student leadership piece reiterates the importance of ensuring that everyone is quiet and listening to the announcements.

Handbooks

School handbooks are also valuable in communicating important aspects of the school. This is a handy tool for students and families to be able to refer to when they need information. Of course, you must adhere to the information that is in it.

Handbooks should include the following items.

- Up-to-date information
- Vision and purpose statements
- Behavior expectations
- Class schedules
- Report card dates
- Extracurricular activities

- Important calendar dates
- Exam schedules and weightings

Your administrative assistant or staff are your go-to people if you're unsure when the handbook was last updated.

Online Messaging

Social media and your school website are timely means of sharing your message. Parents, guardians, and students use their phones for many things, so capitalize on that by ensuring that your school has an online presence. You, your assistant principal, or a dedicated IT staff member need to closely monitor and keep the platforms up to date, or they have no value. Potential and current families will check your website to see what your school is all about. Therefore, it's a great place to share your vision and purpose, the handbook, school calendar, upcoming events, student supply lists, and parent council information, to name a few. Most school districts have a policy and administrative procedure for social media best practices.

Prepare for Tough Conversations

Sometimes, conversations are of a more serious nature. Whether they are with staff, parents or guardians, students, or community members, you should be prepared, know the facts, listen, and maintain positive relationships. The following section focuses on tough conversations with staff; however, the same process and principles apply in any tough conversation.

As much as we all wish for the ideal school where all staff are motivated, skilled, and passionate about teaching, this is rarely the case. Fortunately, most teachers are dedicated and want to do their best. However, there are times when you'll need to have some pertinent conversations with staff who are not meeting the standards that you expect. It is essential to have one-to-one conversations with those individuals as soon as possible.

One principal shared that, while reviewing their instructional work during a staff meeting, two teachers got upset, said some unprofessional things, and walked out of the meeting (C. Bailey, personal communication, October 15, 2024). This is sometimes what principals contend with. The principal kept the meeting on track but knew that the two individuals required individual conversations. The next day, the principal requested to speak with each at a time that was convenient for them. The principal indicated separately to each individual that their actions were unprofessional and inappropriate and would not be tolerated.

Keep the following advice in mind.

- Plan ahead for such conversations.
- Get right to the point.

- Be very specific about what the problem is and what your expectations are for improvement.
- Align improvement expectations with your district and union's expectations.

For example, say a teacher isn't testing students based on the learning outcomes for the course. Be clear in your communication. Ask them, either in person or by email, to meet with you at a specific time and date in your office.

Before the meeting, practice what you want to say and how you want the meeting to go. Run through the conversation, maybe with the assistant principal or a trusted equivalent colleague, to ensure that you are clear and concise. You might say something like the following when you meet with the teacher.

> Teacher A, your exam questions are not covering the required learning outcomes in your course. It is essential to test students on the material they are required to learn. It is my expectation that you review and revise your unit tests to ensure they align with the curricular outcomes. Three days prior to administering another exam, share the exam with me and demonstrate the outcomes that are being tested. If you require assistance or support, let me know. We can work through the next unit test together.

Give the teacher a specified amount of time to complete the next unit test revision and schedule a meeting to review what they have or have not accomplished.

These pertinent conversations are *not* always one and done. Document your actions and those of the teacher. Always ensure that you're providing support to the teacher while maintaining very clear expectations of the desired behaviors.

Final Thoughts: Communication Is Key

As the principal of your school, you are the head cheerleader, so to speak. Students, staff, teachers, families, and your broader community are closely observing your actions, words, and moods. Envision your school as the best and then live up to that by sharing your vision and making decisions that align with that vision. It's intentional work to create the school you envision. Remember that if you don't create the narrative you want, others will happily share another version.

Coherent, consistent, and timely communication is necessary to ensure that all stakeholders are aware of what's happening in the school and that they feel like part of the school community. When everyone feels connected to the school, it creates the conditions to move forward. Use every means possible to share news of the school and to celebrate successes.

Be succinct in your messaging, whether it's an email, a face-to-face meeting, or a newsletter. Keep the message clear so that it isn't lost in all the noise around it. When you need to have a meeting with families, a student, or staff member, get to the meat of the message quickly. Everyone's time is valuable, including yours.

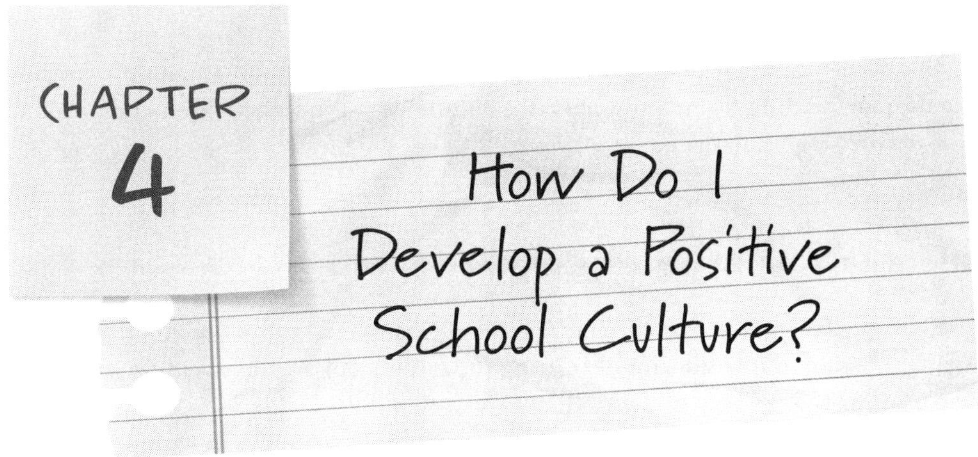

Chapter 4: How Do I Develop a Positive School Culture?

Have you noticed that you can get an immediate sense of the environment when you walk into a school? Does the school feel inviting? This is a strong indication of the type of culture that exists within the walls of a school. It doesn't matter what grade levels are contained within. Do not assume that all elementary schools are warm and welcoming and that all high schools are rigid and uninviting. Culture is complex and influenced by the people within it.

In essence, the culture is a framework and lens through which the school operates. It includes the vision, beliefs, relationships, attitudes, and written and unwritten rules that exist in every building; its history impacts it (Cornell, 2024). A positive school culture is key to greater student and staff achievement, engagement, and motivation.

We don't mean to sound dramatic, but if you do nothing else in your first year as a school principal, you need to ensure you focus on school culture. Research speaks to the benefits of a positive school culture—including students feeling safe, engaged, and supported and promoting their academic, social, emotional, and physical growth (Bozhani, Momeni, & Moradi, 2025; Gruenert & Whitaker, 2015). Positive school culture is key to having high teacher morale and reducing teacher turnover and burnout (Zulqarnain, Ali, & Bashir, 2025). We find that when teachers feel heard, supported, and appreciated, they are more likely to collaborate, learn, take risks to grow, and continue working toward high-quality learning for all students. Conversely, a negative school culture can hinder students' academic, social, emotional, and physical growth and contribute to negative outcomes, such as low attendance, poor academic achievement, and higher dropout rates (Pearson, 2015).

Spending time watching, asking questions, and making decisions leads to learning the explicit (written curriculum) and the more subtle skills and knowledge (hidden curriculum) you need at your school. That takes a long time. To that end, this chapter has an additional element than other chapters in this book. In a series of recurring A Tale of Transforming School Culture boxes, we provide a real-life example of a new principal's journey in transforming school culture. We hope that the journey and the reflective questions provided at the end of each section will support you as you work to transform your school culture.

This chapter will help you identify your school's culture type, determine current cultural strengths and growth areas, align the culture with the school vision and mission, and make that culture visible.

Identify Your School's Culture Type

You must know where you currently are to get where you want to be. You, as the principal, are largely responsible for identifying the existing culture, determining whether it needs to change and how, and modeling how to change it.

Consider these six types of school culture (Deal & Kennedy, 1999; Fullan & Hargreaves, 1996).

1. **Collaborative:** Teachers work together and share the goal and vision of making their school better.
2. **Comfortable-collaborative:** The overall feel is professional; teachers may know what their colleagues are doing, but they do not reflect much on their work or others' work.
3. **Contrived-collegial:** School leadership sets the school's tone, which typically feels superficial to the teachers and results in a lack of motivation.
4. **Balkanized:** Teachers form cliques and compete for resources and control.
5. **Fragmented:** Teachers work in silos, and there is no collaboration regarding best practices or student achievement.
6. **Toxic:** Teachers focus on the negative aspects of their school and colleagues where gossip spreads.

Ultimately, it's ideal to have a collaborative school culture, but that doesn't happen without the intentional work of school leadership. We have been in many schools throughout our careers, and all of these types exist. For the most part, you get a strong sense of the existing culture as soon as you enter the building. Keep an eye out for telltale signs, and keep in mind that staff introductory meetings occur prior to being in the nitty-gritty of full staff meetings and classroom instruction.

A positive culture itself is a need and is foundational to addressing any other need in a school:

> Schools' abilities to improve and sustain effectiveness over the long term are not primarily the result of the principals' leadership style but of their understanding and diagnosis of the school's needs and their application of clearly articulated, organizationally shared educational values through multiple combinations and accumulations of time and context-sensitive strategies that are "layered" and progressively embedded in the school's work, culture, and achievements. (Day, Gu, & Sammons, 2016, pp. 221–222)

We have worked in a high school where the principal had a high level of visibility, engaging with students and staff in the halls. It was obvious that he'd developed a good relationship with students, and the teachers were comfortable with having him in their classrooms. He stopped and chatted with students in their classes to see what they were learning and provided timely feedback to the teachers with an opportunity to meet face to face and discuss how the lesson went.

They happened to be working on cooperative learning strategies as a staff. During staff meetings, the principal shared the data from classroom visits, including the different cooperative learning strategies he observed and the number of classroom visits he completed to garner the data. Teachers took the opportunity to share and discuss both successful and unsuccessful practices they had tried in their classrooms and how they planned to alter their strategies for the next round. It was clear this was a safe environment where teachers were used to sharing their practices and felt comfortable taking risks and engaging in professional discussions.

However, we have visited schools with fragmented and toxic cultures. In one, the staff were divided in two: (1) the individual teachers and (2) the main clique. The clique consisted of a few veteran teachers who were used to having control and making others feel inadequate. The principal and assistant principal were new to the school and intimidated by the group's stronghold. Teachers made unprofessional comments. Students struggled with prosocial, on-task behavior. In our experience, this negative student behavior is common when students have noticed a staff divide. Use these descriptions to see what behaviors and beliefs you observe, then see which type (or types) of cultures exist at your school.

Determine Current Cultural Strengths and Growth Areas

Your school may identify as only one culture type or a couple overlapping types. Using the brief characterizations, collect evidence that supports your initial impression of your culture. For instance, in a collaborative culture, teachers actively engage with one another to plan and improve their practice. If you see evidence that they are using self-reflection and colleague observation, they have moved from the comfortable-collaborative to the full collaborative type. A contrived-collegial culture is where teachers wait to be told what to do and how to do it. In a balkanized culture, you see cliques and certain teachers wielding power over others; many refrain from sharing their opinions and silent looks set the tone. There is no collegial interaction in a fragmented type of culture because teachers are doing their own thing in their own classroom; no one knows or shares what they are doing. A toxic culture is built on complaints; there is never a solution, and teacher isolation is the norm. Use the evidence you collect to move forward in building or maintaining your desired culture.

Even if you are fortunate enough to be taking over a school with a long-held positive school culture, one small change can shake it. It's imperative that you know and understand the core values, beliefs, and traditions—the underlying constructs—that form and support your school culture.

A Tale of Transforming School Culture: Setting the Stage

Ms. Armstrong, one of five candidates for a K–7 school principalship, was excited to participate in a school tour, which was part of the two-day interview process. Upon entering the school on the day of the tour, Ms. Armstrong noticed a long line of students sitting on the floor outside the office. Curious, she asked the administrative assistant what the students were lined up for. Ms. Armstrong was taken aback when the administrative assistant said, "They are lined up for bad behavior and are waiting to see the principal!"

Eventually, Ms. Armstrong was offered the principal position. Based on that day's experience, she already had some insight into the school's culture. She knew her first priority was to find out more about the school's culture and determine how she would need to address it.

How can Ms. Armstrong learn more about her school's culture?

Which of the six types of culture do you see at play here? What evidence supports your choice?

When you first take on the principalship, it is important to remember to "seek first to understand, then to be understood" (Covey, 2020, p. 235). In other words, keep your eyes and ears open and your mouth closed! Be a sponge—all things in your surroundings and interactions will help you gain a deeper understanding of the school's culture.

Discussing these key questions with your staff, students, and families will help you gain an understanding of the culture.

- How are things done around here?
- How do you feel about working here? How do you feel about learning here?
- What needs my immediate attention?
- What are some positive and negative things I need to know about our school?
- What else do I need to know to succeed as the principal of this school?
- Who do you trust and why?
- When you know you need to get something done, who do you ask to get results?

Once you have compiled the answers you receive to these questions, you may want to take them back to your staff, students, and families and ask any additional questions you may have. Ultimately, through this exercise, you want to know what your staff, students, parents, and guardians consider to be the most important aspects of the school culture—what they value and believe in. This will help you determine the cultural strengths and growth areas. Let's look at how Ms. Armstrong addressed this.

A Tale of Transforming School Culture: Assessing the Current Culture

Prior to the school year beginning, Ms. Armstrong met with the staff and families of the school she was now principal of. Staff were concerned about student behavior. They felt a lack of respect permeated the school, and student misbehavior was making it hard to teach. They reported feeling that the previous principal, who had just retired, had mentally checked out years earlier and was just showing up for the paycheck.

Families echoed these concerns and were troubled that the school wasn't a safe or caring place for their students. Those who wanted to volunteer and help in the school and classrooms were turned away. There were very few extracurricular activities for students to participate in. Ms. Armstrong felt she had learned a lot about the school culture by listening to her staff and student families, but she knew it was also important to meet with the students. Ms. Armstrong had recently completed her master's degree focusing on student leadership. During her research project, she had seen the power of providing students not only a voice in their school culture but also the opportunity to lead the work.

What were some of the key themes brought to Ms. Armstrong regarding the school's culture?

What themes do you think students will identify?

Figure 4.1 is a simple visual highlighting some of the differences between a positive and negative school culture. This can be a quick reference for you when you begin to determine where your school culture is.

Positive School Culture	Negative School Culture
★ **Vision and mission:** They are shared among stakeholders, and everyone owns them.	★ **Vision and mission:** They belong to the principal alone; there is no shared ownership.
★ **Relationships:** They are positive.	★ **Relationships:** They are strained or individualistic.
★ **Collegiality:** We are in this together, and this is our school. Let's collaborate on this.	★ **Collegiality:** It is lacking. There are cliques and loners. People think, "We can do this our way, and this is my classroom."
★ **Leadership:** All voices matter and everyone has strengths.	★ **Leadership:** There is one leader and one voice.
★ **Clarity:** Everyone knows the work that is being done.	★ **Clarity:** It is lacking. There is chaos. Everyone has their own understanding of what to do.

Figure 4.1: Positive versus negative school culture.

continued ▶

Positive School Culture	Negative School Culture
★ **Behavior:** Everyone has participated in the development and models the expectations. Positive behavior is taught, modeled, and reinforced.	★ **Behavior:** It is addressed inconsistently. Staff ignore misbehavior. The school feels unsafe.
★ **Professional learning:** High-quality professional learning is provided to staff and students. There is positive risk taking.	★ **Professional learning:** The group agrees that they should keep doing it the way they have always done it.
★ **Celebrations:** Successes are recognized and promote the work of all stakeholders.	★ **Celebrations:** They only recognize certain individuals and create resentment.
★ **Expectations and support:** Expectations and support are high.	★ **Expectations and support:** There are low or no expectations and support.

Align Culture With the School Vision and Mission

Culture impacts everything in a school, making it imperative that it aligns with your vision and mission. Your vision and mission inform how you collaboratively set your school norms and the expectations that will support your school's social, emotional, and physical safety. It is foundational for developing a positive school culture. However, you must know where you are before you can begin shaping that culture. Again, it is important to consult the six types of school culture as a starting point.

There is no specific recipe for this work—your context is unique—but there are some overall strategies. Begin by gathering information regarding the values, perceptions, history, and beliefs of staff, students, and families. It's time to act. As mentioned, you can take this information back to each group and confirm that what you've heard truly represents what they shared. Then, ensure alignment between your school vision and values. Staff commitment (page 8) and ownership of both vision and values are key to staff actively participating.

The following strategies can help: embracing consistency, engaging stakeholders, sharing leadership, reviewing and reinforcing what you value, supporting culture with data, and celebrating students and staff.

A Tale of Transforming School Culture: Seeing Vision in the Foundation

Ms. Armstrong's district hosted three staff days prior to the start of school. Half of these days provided principals time to set the direction for the upcoming school year with their staff. The remaining time focused on district-mandated professional learning opportunities. Ms. Armstrong knew she had to plan well and use this time to build a strong, positive school culture. The staff focused on developing their vision and mission during the first half of the day.

They didn't complete the mission and vision, but they had a clear understanding of what they all valued. Learning for all students; a safe, welcoming, and caring environment; and a responsive and equitable culture were some of the key ideas coming out of the vision and mission work. Ms. Armstrong wanted to spend the next half of the day focusing on behavior, as she knew that a safe and welcoming school was necessary to achieve all the values they had just discussed.

During her years as a classroom teacher, Ms. Armstrong had worked in schools where behavior was addressed by teachers on their own, or students were sent to the office. Consequences for behavior differed in scope and severity. These methods resulted in learning environments that were unpredictable and unsafe. However, she had also worked in schools with a common understanding and a commitment to consistent consequences. This resulted in a positive culture.

What was some of Ms. Armstrong's foundational work toward creating a positive school culture?

How have you used your school vision to create a positive culture?

Embrace Consistency

Consistency is crucial when you're working on school culture and regularly reinforcing this work throughout your day. Research indicates that "consistency usually feels positive," which increases trust (Nowak, Biesaga, Ziembowicz, Baran, & Winkielman, 2023). All actions, behaviors, and words must be consistent with your school vision. Trust, respect, staff and student growth, and success all depend on this.

Behavior expectations must be the same for everyone. We have been in schools and witnessed staff publicly berating a student for disrespectful behavior. Publicly addressing a student's behavior does *not* model respect. Privately addressing behavior allows students to maintain their dignity and supports them in learning from the mistake.

Engage Stakeholders

Stakeholder involvement is also key. Positive relationships are the foundation of a strong school culture (Durham et al., 2017). Staff, students, and families need to feel valued, respected, heard, and cared for. You can read about building relationships with these groups in chapter 2 (page 15).

These groups have ownership when they are involved in identifying what is valued and in the branding of these values. We have been in schools where the culture is so positive that if a new student joins the school, their fellow students inculcate them with their culture. They don't want their positive learning environment changed!

Share Leadership

Shared leadership, which we'll also discuss in chapter 7 (page 93), deepens the commitment of all stakeholders to your vision, mission, and positive school culture (Goddard, Hoy, & Hoy, 2000; Hughes & Morrison, 2022). We make the point throughout this book that the learning environment that students need cannot be accomplished by the principal alone. Sharing leadership also helps build strong and trusting relationships. You can share leadership with all stakeholders, and it can cover any aspects of school life depending on their interests and strengths. Trust others to help lead but verify that they are accomplishing what they are tasked with.

Shared leadership approaches in schools that distribute responsibility can enhance motivation, foster authentic trust, encourage risk taking, and cultivate a sense of community and effectiveness among members:

> Principals that allow all team members, from custodial and kitchen staff to teachers and support staff, to make positive contributions to the school community, while holding those who deter a positive school culture accountable, will foster a high-quality working environment for staff and an excellent learning environment for students. (Murray, 2025)

A Tale of Transforming School Culture: Sharing Leadership

Ms. Armstrong met with the grades 6 and 7 students in her school. She knew that, as the oldest students in the building, they had the ability to positively or negatively impact the school culture. They reviewed the new school mantra and behavior norms together. Ms. Armstrong asked the students if they thought the school should change somehow. Students asked if they could enter the building at a different entrance than the younger students. They didn't want to have to wait until the younger students were inside. Ms. Armstrong said she thought that was something they could change, but she would have to run it by the staff as well.

One student asked why picking up garbage was used as a punishment for misbehavior. Ms. Armstrong asked why they were asking. The student replied that if they truly believed they were respecting the environment, there shouldn't be any garbage on the playground. If there was, they should be picking it up to create a positive school environment, not picking it up because they were being disciplined. Ms. Armstrong said she was in total agreement and would let everyone know that picking up garbage was a valued behavior and that it demonstrated respect for the environment.

Next, Ms. Armstrong asked the students to take the lead on teaching the behavior matrix to the younger students. The matrix outlined what values looked, felt, and sounded like in all areas of the school. They organized stations for each area of the school that the behavior matrix addressed. In groups, they planned a lesson and a game for their stations. They worked with her to prepare the lessons, and when they were ready, they hosted the stations.

What do you see as the most positive outcome of Ms. Armstrong having students lead this work?

In what ways have you involved students in building a positive culture in your school?

Review and Reinforce What You Value

Building school culture needs to be intentional, modeled, and taught—and not just once. You need to regularly review and reinforce what you value in your school culture. Many principals use their daily announcements to review behavior expectations and their school's values. For example, a high school principal can greet students in the main hallway and commend them on the behaviors that match school expectations. Another example is keeping the learning and physical work environment well maintained. Are there papers hanging out of lockers and trash on the floors? Make it clear that everyone is expected to play a role in keeping the school neat and tidy.

Consider a school that has a staff committee responsible for teaching the expected behaviors featured in their behavior matrix. They have planning time for lessons that they can adapt to different grade levels. Often, they teach and reteach these lessons before reviewing with students. Additionally, school assemblies, newsletters (page 44), and positive phone calls home (page 25) are ways to reinforce and build a strong, positive school culture.

Set high expectations for your students, teachers, and support staff (Cornell, 2024; Wilson, n.d.). This expectation relates directly to students' behaviors and academic achievement and teacher behaviors and instruction. Of course, it's critical that you also adhere to the high expectations you have set for everyone else. As mentioned, you convey this by respecting and appreciating the value of others, sharing decision making, listening to and acting on behalf of all stakeholders, and maintaining a positive demeanor when dealing with student discipline or staff performance evaluations.

Making sure you provide support is another way to model a positive culture. Students need access to high-quality teaching, and teachers need access to high-quality resources and professional learning opportunities. Resources do not just apply to things that can be purchased. Tap into free, accessible, undervalued resources, including family volunteers, teacher and principal networks, and community partners. If a resource feels too expensive, time consuming, or scarce to procure, you'll have to use your listening skills and problem-solving strategies to address their needs.

Support Culture With Data

In all your work to achieve the vision and mission in your school, remember that data is your friend. Even in the work relating to your school culture, you need to use data to measure its impact. Staff, students, and families need to see data and understand what it tells them about the impact of the work you're all doing in the school. When stakeholders collaborate to analyze student data, they can make informed decisions based on current evidence rather than relying on opinions, assumptions, or unsubstantiated perspectives.

These are examples of data to gather.

- Attendance
- Office referrals (with subsections)
- Names of who addressed a behavior
- Locations of identified misbehavior (such as restrooms)
- Accidents or injuries
- Parent and guardian contacts

If you see that most student misbehavior is in the washroom, then you would need to add additional supervision or a tracking system for washroom visits. If the data shows that attendance is an issue when it hasn't been on teachers' radars, then sharing the data and determining why certain behaviors are occurring belongs to all educators.

Regardless of whom you're sharing data with, your school vision is at the center of any decision making based on it. When presenting data to any group, provide the full picture while maintaining confidentiality.

A Tale of Transforming School Culture: Using Data

Ms. Armstrong knew that the work had a positive impact on school culture—so much so that her parent council asked if the school could develop a behavior matrix for home! Ms. Armstrong let them know that this was work they had to do at home with their own children, but she reviewed what they had done to develop the school matrix and provided the families with a blank matrix they could use for their homework.

Ms. Armstrong knew that data was necessary to show the positive impact they were having in their work on school culture. The staff had agreed to track behavior referrals to the office. The tracking system separated behaviors in relation to areas such as disrespect, bathroom behavior, lateness, swearing, fighting, and more. Behavior reports also tracked if the behavior had been addressed by a teacher or the principal. Staff had also committed to recognizing positive student behavior by acknowledging it with a paper award. These simple paper awards outlined the behavior the student had displayed.

Additional data was collected through classroom walkthroughs, observations, and surveys. At their monthly staff meetings, Ms. Armstrong and the staff would review all the data and plan their next steps in their positive school culture work.

Why did Ms. Armstrong have staff recognize positive behavior?

In what ways are you using data to positively impact your school culture?

Celebrate Students and Staff

A positive school culture needs to be celebrated, and celebrating successes reinforces a positive school culture. The success of both students and staff needs to be recognized. When you recognize your teachers, they are more likely to feel valued and will be more motivated to continue the work (Hierck, Coleman, & Weber, 2011). When you recognize your students, you reinforce all of the positive things they are doing. Many schools give students tickets, which they can redeem for prizes, when someone has seen them displaying a positive behavior. Staff can also receive tickets, and the newsletter is a good place to recognize staff who are doing positive work.

A Tale of Transforming School Culture: Celebrating

Her first year as principal was almost at an end. Ms. Armstrong had just spent her last staff professional learning day reviewing their data and their successes for the year. Office referrals were almost nil; students were well behaved and happy to be at school. School survey data reflected that all stakeholders felt the school was safe and welcoming. Overall academics had improved. Staff meetings were focusing more on teacher practice than student behavior. There were a lot of things to celebrate.

When asked what they valued and why their school was demonstrating such marked improvement, all stakeholders' replies contained the same key responses. One staff member was retiring, and fellow staff members had already volunteered to meet with her replacement to introduce them to the school's culture and explain how things worked. There were still things to do, but with their school vision, mission, and behavior expectations all consistently understood and practiced, it was easier to identify growth areas.

They had completed their draft school plan, and staff had volunteered for leadership roles on the committees that had been created to support their work. The sixth-grade students were excited to be the seventh-grade heads of the student leadership committee and were excited to train their new sixth-grade peers. Several student-transfer requests from parents waited for Ms. Armstrong on her desk. Her school was gaining a reputation in the community as a great place to learn. That weekend, Ms. Armstrong was hosting her staff for a year-end barbeque. It was time to celebrate!

What parts of the school culture should be maintained and deepened?

What work is positively impacting your school culture?

Make the Culture Visible

As we discussed in chapter 3 (page 35), some schools have branded what they value through the creation of a mantra and norms. Steve Bollar (2025), K–12 climate and culture specialist, states that "defining your values isn't enough . . . [You must] make them visible and part of your school's daily routine."

In chapter 1, we examined the importance of everyone having the same understanding of the words in the school vision. We often ask principals whose schools have mantras and norms, "If we asked all your stakeholders what these looked, sounded, and felt like in your building, would everyone give the same answer?" If their response is not a resounding "yes," there is most likely more work to accomplish in relation to culture. This may be the time to return to the six types of school culture (page 50), pull the data you collected, identify where you are, and plan your next steps. This might be as simple as ensuring your messaging is clear and concise. It may mean it is time to review your vision or behavior matrix. In addition, bulletin boards displaying student work and murals help make norms, expectations, and celebrations visible (Gruenert & Whitiker, 2015). Assemblies and recognition programs are also ways to share school values and celebrate student and staff achievements (Kouzes & Posner, 2017).

A Tale of Transforming School Culture: Making It Visible

Ms. Armstrong and her staff had an extremely productive afternoon looking at and drafting out a school mantra and behavior expectations. They had a draft mantra and acronym: "At our school, we will RAISE learning to the highest heights."

RAISE stood for the following.

- Respect
- All
- Individuals
- Self
- Environment

The staff also worked together to create a behavior matrix. (They later added a community piece for field trips and the like.) Ms. Armstrong made sure staff understood that everyone would follow it and their next step was to bring this work to their students and families to garner their input. They would make posters and lessons once everything was finalized.

Why is it important for families and students to have input?

How have you included your staff, parents, guardians, and students in the development of your school culture?

Final Thoughts: Culture Is Key

A positive school culture is a fragile thing. It is not a one-time or one-year event. It is an ongoing process that requires dedication, hard work, and a commitment to your school vision and mission. It can easily be disrupted if the principal alone tries to maintain it. Everyone in the school is responsible for the culture. To ensure its stability, you need to keep your school vision at the core. It needs to be modeled and visible. What you value needs to be so clear that anyone new to the school can easily understand what is expected and how things are done. Principals and staff should be able to answer when asked to explain how your culture was built and how you will maintain it. Otherwise, a positive culture exists on shaky ground.

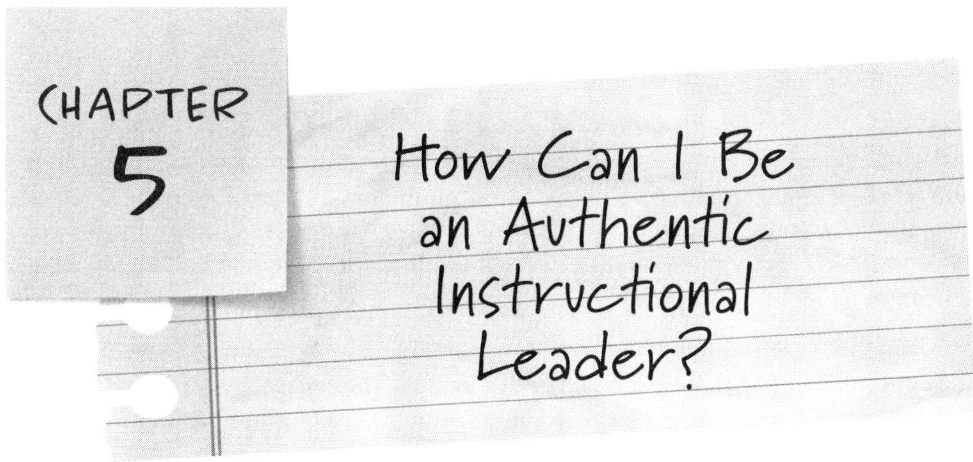

Next to the classroom teacher, principals have the greatest impact on student learning (Grissom et al., 2021). You will find your greatest influence lies in your instructional leadership practices. *Instructional leadership* intentionally supports the development of teaching and learning (Le Fevre, 2019). Indeed, instructional leadership—any strategies you use to improve teaching and learning—is a vital aspect of effective educational leadership. Your instructional leadership practices will impact both your teachers' and students' success.

This chapter examines the following practices. Prioritizing them ensures that your approach to instructional leadership has positive impact.

- Establish a strong focus on learning for all students.
- Set clear goals.
- Make data-informed decisions.
- Support teachers through supervision and evaluation.
- Promote collaboration.
- Engage with stakeholders.

These practices protect teachers and students from distractions and keep the focus on high-quality teaching and learning. This responsibility may seem huge, but the good news is instructional leadership can be shared with and enacted by others, and we will examine this in more depth in chapter 7 (page 93). By focusing on these leadership practices, you will be able to support the development of teaching and learning in your school, which ultimately improves student success and builds an environment of continuous improvement.

Establish a Strong Focus on Learning for All Students

There are several ways to establish a strong focus on learning for all students, including having high expectations, being a lead learner, protecting staff instructional time, and prioritizing improved teaching and learning.

Have High Expectations

As the instructional leader in your school, you need to have the belief that your school, students, and staff can perform at high levels. That commitment impacts student learning (Deal & Peterson, 2016). There is a commonly retold story about a new teacher who had been given one of the lowest-achieving classes in the school. When that teacher started the year, the principal gave them the class list with all the students' names and a number beside each one. At the end of the year, the principal popped in to go over the teacher's evaluation and debrief the year with them. The principal commented on how well the students had done and how amazed he was. The teacher was surprised by these comments. The teacher said that they felt like they had only supported the students in achieving what they were capable of. The principal questioned this statement.

The teacher explained that the principal had provided the students' names and IQ scores at the beginning of the year so the teacher knew they could achieve at a high level. The principal gasped at her explanation and said, "Those weren't their IQs. They were their locker numbers." Ah, the power of high expectations. Whether this is just an urban myth or a true story, it certainly points to the fact that we truly believe our teachers and students will achieve at high levels when given the right supports and conditions. What supports and conditions should you have in place? Every student and adult in your school needs to feel like they belong, that they are safe, and that you have their best interests at heart. They need to know that, even though your expectations are high, you will be there to provide them with the resources and support to help them achieve their goals.

Having high expectations for your school is equal parts belief and action (Prendergast & Lee, 2024). You cannot have one without the other. You also need to have high expectations for yourself. You will need to model the behaviors and learning achievements you set for your students and staff. In other words, "Your actions speak louder than words," and "What you permit, you promote."

Be a Lead Learner

To build a strong focus on learning for all, you must first see yourself as the lead learner. What do we mean when we say lead learner? Being a lead learner isn't something you can proclaim. It is something that is lived. Being the lead learner means you will need to demonstrate a commitment to lifelong learning by always looking to improve, keeping up to date on the latest research and practices, and sharing these findings with your staff and colleagues.

Lead learners create an environment that encourages exploration, innovation, and risk taking for themselves and their staff, who then have high expectations for their students. Making connections is also critical, per former principal Joe Mazza:

> For instance, "If my staff doesn't have someone really strong in literacy, I need to be connected, at the click of a button on my phone, to the person who has researched the topic or led great

> lessons around it." It's "about building [up] the people around you to be constantly learning with you." (as cited in McKibben, 2015)

Lead learners know that they cannot be the expert in everything. Instead, they thrive on collaboration, promoting an environment where everyone believes that they are better together. They encourage others to take ownership of their learning and set learning goals. This certainly overlaps with professional development, but the message here is learning is constant and collaborative. Lead learners value feedback and engage in the kinds of deeper learning that lead to growth. This is visible in the classroom when teachers model high expectations and learning for everyone.

Feedback and reflection are visible in the classroom when teachers do the following (Prendergast & Lee, 2024).

- Believe all of their students can learn.
- Understand that their instructional strategies are a pathway to supporting student success.
- Understand that they might need to break some learning outcomes into smaller sections.
- Believe that they will do whatever it takes to support all students to be successful.

Ultimately, as the lead learner, you reflect a true love for teaching and learning.

Protect Staff Instructional Time

One way you can reflect this true love for teaching and learning is to protect instructional time for staff. There are so many distractions that compete for attention in schools. As we have mentioned, you and your staff should make every decision through the lens of the school vision. Is another entertainment group going to impact student success, or do we need to spend more time as a collaborative team discussing research-backed classroom practices that are engaging and impactful?

Prioritize Improved Teaching and Learning

Another way to reflect lifetime learning is prioritizing your time so your work focuses on improving teaching and learning in your school. Just like a classroom teacher has a day planner, you should as well. This will help keep your focus on your instructional leadership priorities and allow you to plan for the more managerial aspects of your work. Keep notes on how things unfolded or changed for each part of every day. A sample day may look like the one in figure 5.1 (page 66). The notes in italics indicate each action's focus.

	Monday	Notes, Reflections, and Reminders
7:30–8:15	Arrive, check schedule, answer emails, and prepare for the day. *(Ensuring your school day focuses on supporting teachers and students)*	Reschedule Friday assembly to the afternoon; let staff and student leaders know.
8:15–8:45	Meet with the assistant principal to review any items we both need to be aware of or follow up on. *(Building their capacity and modeling strong communication skills)*	Book substitute teacher for Friday to support me with the professional learning plan.
8:45–9:00	Greet students by name as they enter the building. Monitor the building to ensure teachers and staff are prepared for the day. *(Tending to relationships)*	Checked in with Tina; she didn't seem like her regular cheery self this morning.
9:00–9:15	Supervise student announcers as they give the daily announcements and reminders. *(Building student leadership skills)*	Book the next pairing of student announcers for next week.
9:15–9:30	Touch base with our special education teacher to ensure she has the new resources the district is providing. *(Meeting all students' needs)*	Observe her during the morning block next week.
9:30–10:30	Conduct classroom walkthroughs: • Grade 6, Smith—Formative Assessment • Grade 7, Hicks—Behavior, Sarah and Tatiana • Grade 8, Brown—Transitions *(Using instructional leadership)*	See walkthrough binder for feedback notes. Smith and Hicks debriefs are today.
10:30–10:45	Help with recess supervision: grade 8 hallway. *(Tending to relationships and ensuring a safe, caring environment)*	Grade 8 meeting: Students and staff review and practice hallway expectations tomorrow morning.
10:45–11:45	Attend grade 6 humanities team meeting. Review and revise norms, present and discuss social studies unit 1 common assessment data, and plan next steps. *(Building teacher capacity and meeting all students' needs)*	Revised norms are ready to be published. Share next-steps plan with assistant principal.

11:45–1:00	Have lunch with the student leadership team. Review monthly character focus. Plan for the team to lead Friday's assembly. Touch base with assistant principal to see how their morning went. *(Building relationships, supporting student leadership and ownership, and planning forward with assistant principal)*	Let staff know respect will be the character focus for the month. School assembly practice with student leadership team on Thursday during last block—let teachers of those students know.
1:00–1:45	Meet with assistant to go over the school resource account. Review expectations for welcoming people into the building. *(Using resources effectively for school operations and maintenance)*	Continue monitoring resource account.
1:45–2:30	Meet with custodian David to resolve issue with boot mats; replace them with something more durable. Debrief classroom walkthrough with Mr. Smith. Plan next steps with formative assessment strategies. *(Ensuring a safe, caring environment and showing instructional leadership)*	Contact district maintenance office to see if they know of a more durable carpet, and will they cover the cost? Plan next walkthrough date.
2:30–3:15	Meet with the district literacy coordinator to discuss their presentation at our next professional learning day. Provide our staff profile and determine how to differentiate the presentation to meet all of their learning needs. *(Pursuing professional learning, showing instructional leadership, and meeting staff learning needs)*	See professional learning binder for updated plan; have admin assistant draft that day's agenda.
3:15–3:30	Help with bus supervision. *(Tending to relationships and ensuring a safe, caring environment)*	Review the loading of students on buses with transportation. Would it make more sense for south bus to leave first?
3:30–4:00	Debrief classroom walkthrough with Mr. Hicks, including possible behavior plans for students. Meet with Mrs. Brown tomorrow before classes. *(Showing instructional leadership and meeting staff and student needs)*	See walkthrough binder.
4:00–4:30	Call parents of S.C. to arrange a meeting regarding absence, and return emails to parents. *(Tending to relationships and meeting student needs)*	Finish on Wednesday at 8:15 a.m.

Figure 5.1: Example day planner.

Tips to Thrive

It is important that your administrative assistant knows your plan and understands that its purpose is paramount in your instructional leadership work. For example, when you are conducting classroom walkthroughs, your administrative assistant should know to say something like, "The principal is not currently in their office. They are in classrooms supporting teachers and students in their learning." You might also put this message on your personal voicemail. The message is clear: Teaching and learning are your focus.

Set Clear Goals

As the principal and instructional leader in your school, it will be very important to have a few specific, measurable goals to guide your vision. Goals provide a clear direction, which allows you and your staff to prioritize tasks and avoid getting sidetracked. They also establish benchmarks that make it easier to track your progress and identify areas where you might need to alter your approach. Note that data is an important piece in setting the right goals. You can't have clear goals without data, and we'll touch on data in the next section.

Ultimately, the purpose of setting goals is to reach your intended outcome. Collaborating with staff in setting clear, measurable goals is a critical leadership practice that can significantly impact student success (Robinson, 2011). When staff are included in the goal-setting process, they feel a sense of ownership, a purpose, and a direction in which to go.

Many school districts provide beginning-of-the-year planning days in their school calendars. Principals can work with their school teams on these days to develop their goals and how they will address them. Most districts also require school principals to share their goals (improvement plans) with their parent council. One principal we worked with, Mr. Hall, was very intentional about how he walked his parent council through their planning process. He sought feedback from the parents and guardians and provided further explanations to ensure they truly understood the work. These participants are a collective voice in the community; ensure that the message is clear and in family-friendly language.

There is an abundance of resources available regarding goal setting. Author Peter DeWitt (2017) outlines a user-friendly cycle for goal setting in *Collaborative Leadership: Six Influences That Matter Most.* Authors Lindsay Prendergast and Piper Lee (2024) provide a full chapter in their book *Habits of Resilient Educators: Strategies for Thriving During Times of Anxiety, Doubt, and Constant Change* that discusses the importance of goals and steps for setting them. It is important to seek support and mentorship if you need it. Continuing with goals that were set the previous year and with the previous principal distances you from being part of the collaboration necessary for everyone to own the work. Setting and achieving goals can only be accomplished when it is done in a collaborative learning culture. Goals need to be created, understood, and enacted with a shared commitment to the result and the effort, work, and professional growth required to achieve them.

Make Data-Informed Decisions

The education field doesn't lack data. Being data informed helps us, as educators, act on facts rather than assumptions. By using data, you and your staff will be able to determine where student learning gaps exist, where teacher practice needs to improve, and which strategies will best address each variable. As the principal, you need to create an atmosphere where data isn't feared and is regularly used to inform your next steps to meet both student and staff needs.

You can create (or sustain) this data-informed culture through the following efforts.

- Ensure teachers know what data you collect and why and can use it to inform their own work, a team's work, or the entire school's work. For example, literacy assessment data can point teachers to additional strategies they need to employ.
- Provide teachers with easy access to the data. For example, ensure there are visuals, such as the district dashboard and staff training, on how to interpret data effectively.
- Encourage open communication with staff about what their data indicates and the implications. For example, a high school cross-departmental collaboration can lead to richer insights and a shared understanding of how students succeed in different areas. (For instance, using history class data, they can determine that students are struggling with reading charts, which leads to the mathematics teacher spending additional time on this in their class.)
- Encourage staff to collaborate, evaluate progress, learn from outcomes, and plan next steps for improvement. Ensure they get collaborative time during staff meetings and professional learning. Part of those efforts include reviewing how to interpret data.

Tips to Thrive

Mr. Grath, principal of a K–12 school, organized his staff into multigrade groups when they looked at their school data. One of the twelfth-grade humanities teachers commented on how much he learned from his kindergarten-teacher colleague when looking at the data. This process also promoted a full-staff conversation on what each grade needed to cover to ensure all students successfully graduate high school.

All of us have had to learn to become comfortable with data. We have sought support from our district office staff and colleagues and participated in professional learning sessions. It takes time and practice but is well worth it; it's necessary for us to make educational decisions based on facts not feelings. Building a data-informed culture is an important process that requires commitment from all staff. As principal, taking collaborative steps and prioritizing data-informed decision making will positively impact teacher growth and student success.

Support Teachers Through Supervision and Evaluation

As the principal and instructional leader, you will provide several ways for your staff to achieve at high levels. Teacher supervision is key for supporting your teachers in improving their practice, reflecting, and meeting your high expectations. It is important for you to understand that teacher supervision is separate from teacher evaluation. There are many different terms to describe the teacher supervision process, such as classroom walkthroughs, coaching trios, or instructional rounds. All these complete the supervision process in a different way.

No matter what the process is called, plan and set aside time to do the following.

- Provide support, guidance, and reflective feedback to teachers.
- Observe and receive information from a variety of sources about the quality of teaching your teachers are providing to their students.
- Identify any teacher behaviors or practices that would require a formal evaluation process.

The supervision you provide should be intentional, planned, and differentiated to meet the needs of each member of your teaching staff. In the beginning stages of your principalship, you will get to know your staff's strengths and growth opportunities in several ways, such as individual introduction meetings, growth plan meetings, classroom visits, and walkthroughs. We see classroom visits and walkthroughs as two separate data collection tools.

Classroom visits are usually very short. During this time, you certainly can gather data, such as how the students are engaging in the lesson, the feel of the room, general routines, and so on. However, during a classroom walkthrough—even if it's just ten minutes—you can take notes, focus on a particular area of instruction (could be chosen by yourself or the teacher), and prepare to meet with the teacher after to debrief the visit in a manner that helps the teacher reflect on their practice and determine next steps in their growth.

Many principals provide feedback to their teachers through email. We prefer to follow up with a face-to-face meeting. During this meeting, share facts you observed while conducting your walkthrough and ask reflective questions that help the teacher determine the next steps in the supervision process. All districts have a teacher standard for both supervision and evaluation. Sticking to the competencies in the standard will support you in this work. A few resources clearly outline the supervision process, including Justin Baeder's (2018) *Now We're Talking! 21 Days to High-Performance Instructional Leadership*. We also find that practicing the conversation with a trusted colleague, such as your assistant principal, will help you build confidence and skill.

As we have described, supervision is a collaborative process by which principals observe and gather information to support, guide, and provide professional growth opportunities for teachers. However, if any information collected during your supervision process gives you reason to believe that a teacher isn't meeting their professional competencies, you would move to a formal evaluation. Additional reasons for a formal evaluation process follow.

- Accommodating a teacher's request
- Gathering information related to a specific teaching position
- Assessing teacher growth in relation to a particular teaching competency

Your school district will have a policy regarding teacher evaluation, and it's important that you understand what is expected in this process. The format in which the evaluation is written will also be included in the policy. If you are unsure about any aspect of the evaluation process, ask for help from your district human resources staff. Conducting a formal teacher evaluation is never easy, but it is important to remember that you are one of several gatekeepers of the profession and have the future of your most precious resource—your students—in your hands.

Promote Collaboration

Looking back on the most successful events in our careers, we quickly realize that these successes were not achieved on our own. Education has become more complex, and we have learned that the problems we face can be solved more successfully when we collaborate. Case in point, this book has four authors, and we truly believe that our collaboration will provide abundant experience to support you in your role as principal.

Collaboration, in the simplest definition, means working together. We wish it was that easy, but as we know, even when we ask our students to collaborate, we need to have routines and structures and teach them *how* to collaborate. The same can be said for staff collaboration. As principal, you will need to have routines and model how collaboration happens. In chapter 4 (page 49), we looked at how you develop a positive school culture that supports collaborative structures. In this section, we will look at how your instructional leadership promotes and supports collaboration.

It is important to note that research shows that collaboration among teachers is key to promoting a positive and effective educational environment (Darling-Hammond, Hyler, & Gardner, 2017; Hargreaves & Fullan, 2012). When staff share ideas and practices, it leads to improved student outcomes and overall school performance. Building a sense of teamwork through collaboration fosters a sense of community, trust, and open communication, making teachers feel valued and supported. Through sharing experiences and successes, teachers can combat feelings of isolation and stress, enhancing their mental well-being and efficacy. Just like your students, your teachers have unique strengths. Providing time for collaboration allows them to leverage each other's skills.

As discussed in chapter 4, there needs to be trust for collaboration to work. Your words and actions will be key to laying the foundation. You are contributing to a culture of trust when you support your words with actions, develop strong professional relationships, and model humility and lifelong learning.

How can you, as the instructional leader, support collaboration in your school? Here are just a few suggestions we have seen during our time working in schools and with educators.

- You cannot overcommunicate to your staff that given the right support and through collaboration, they can close the gap.
- Provide time for collaboration during the school day, meetings, and professional learning opportunities.
- Make data accessible and understandable so it can inform collaboration.
- Teach discussion and decision-making skills.

Mrs. Gatteman, an elementary principal, was very intentional about supporting teachers in working collaboratively. She had modeled many of the structures for collaboration through staff meetings and professional learning sessions. When she believed staff were ready, she built in time for grade-alike staff to collaborate. For these collaborative meetings, one staff member was chosen by their peers to be the lead. The lead was responsible for setting the agenda for their collaboration time and sharing the meeting results with Mrs. Gatteman.

These collaborative session agendas focused on a problem of practice that grade-alike teachers had identified and were learning about. Mrs. Gatteman provided these collaboration times in the schedule a few ways. Some blocks were available due to Mrs. Gatteman taking all the students from the grade to the gym for games, soft skills learning, and guest speakers. Sometimes, time was available because the students were in a library block, and an additional staff member could provide added supervision.

There are a variety of instructionally sound ways to make room for staff to collaborate. There are also many things staff can collaborate on. However, it is important to remember that working together is not enough unless it results in improvements for students—improved teacher instruction and student achievement.

Engage With Stakeholders

Although we have several different stakeholder groups in terms of instructional leadership, this section focuses on students, families, district staff, and community members—your stakeholders.

Students

Your students not only need a strong instructional leader, but they also need to be engaged in some of the decisions that are being made regarding their learning. Being visible in classrooms and around the school demonstrates to your students that you are interested and care about what they are learning. Giving them a voice on these matters provides further proof of this. You can engage them in school decisions via a student advisory team or a student leadership team.

How you form the group and determine what decisions they are charged with are unique to you and your school context. In our experience, all students, even as early as kindergarten, can be part of a student leadership group or initiative. In some schools, the group is organized by one representative per grade who students choose. Some other schools have the oldest students form the group but then garner feedback from lower grades. Similar to staff meetings, students develop norms, and all meetings have an agenda. Students we have worked with who have participated in these groups report a better understanding of how decisions are made in the school, that they play a big part in creating a positive school culture, and that their opinions matter.

Families

Research shows that families who build strong efficacy with their children's educational lives can make a huge difference in the degree to which their children are successful in school (Constantino, 2021). How parents and guardians feel about your school is ultimately how the broader community will perceive it.

As we discussed in chapter 3 (page 35), you cannot overcommunicate all the great work you are doing in your school, and your family community will be some of your best advocates. You can engage families in a multitude of ways to inform them of the great work happening in your school.

- **Share your school-improvement plans with families:** The following details can be the difference between families feeling engaged and indifferent.
    - Use family-friendly language.
    - Share the data that informs the plan.
    - Share how you will work to achieve the plan.
    - Revisit the plan regularly to share progress.

- **Carefully plan school events:** Determine how the event can also be a forum for sharing information about the work you're doing. School assemblies are one possibility; consider putting information such as special events and successes on the back of the assembly program. This information would have already appeared in a newsletter or over the announcements. Some might argue that assemblies take away from instructional time, which is why—just like staff meetings—it's important everyone understands the assembly's purpose and how it supports the school's work.

Engaging with every family can be difficult. Try the following strategies to address this issue (Regional Educational Laboratory, 2021).

- Use two-way communication versus only pushing out information.
- Codevelop goals that you share with students.
- Address things that hinder family-school partnerships (including event timing and language differences).
- Work to understand families in the school community.
- Create ways for families to engage with and support other families, which can include hosting informal gatherings.

The key is to approach families in an asset-based, culturally sensitive way and ensure that the ways you loop them in are systemwide, a part of all strategies, and sustained (Mapp & Bergman, 2019; Mapp & Kuttner, 2013).

District Staff

When district staff—including the superintendent, directors, coaches, and more—are in your school, showcase the great work that is happening. Student ambassadors can welcome visitors to the building and give a short tour highlighting the school vision, behavior matrixes, and displayed student work. They can also give a short presentation on a leadership project they are involved in. As principal, you know what is best for this occasion.

Broader Community

Sharing school information with the broader community can take many forms. Inviting community members to important school events and attending community events that are relevant to your school will build the community's understanding of your school's vision and the work being done in relation to it. As a result, they'll become advocates and share your successes with others. You have a lot on your plate in the first year of your new position. Many of the researched ideas for involving the broader community would mirror those that involve families. You can get into the specifics of this when you feel more comfortable with all the other topics covered in this book.

Final Thoughts: Instructional Leadership Means Continuous Learning

As the instructional leader in your school, you will need to have a strong focus on learning for all students and staff. A positive, collaborative school culture is the foundation on which your instructional leadership work will happen. When you set clear goals, have high expectations for all (including yourself), and are data informed, you are an instructional leader.

Quality professional learning, examined in the following chapter, is key to building your teachers' skills, and their growth needs to be supported through your completion of regular classroom walkthroughs. We also discussed what you will need to do if you have evidence that a teacher is not meeting their professional competencies. Engaging with your stakeholders is also a key leadership practice. Your stakeholders are one source with which to share the great news about all the gains you are making in relation to teacher growth, student learning, and success.

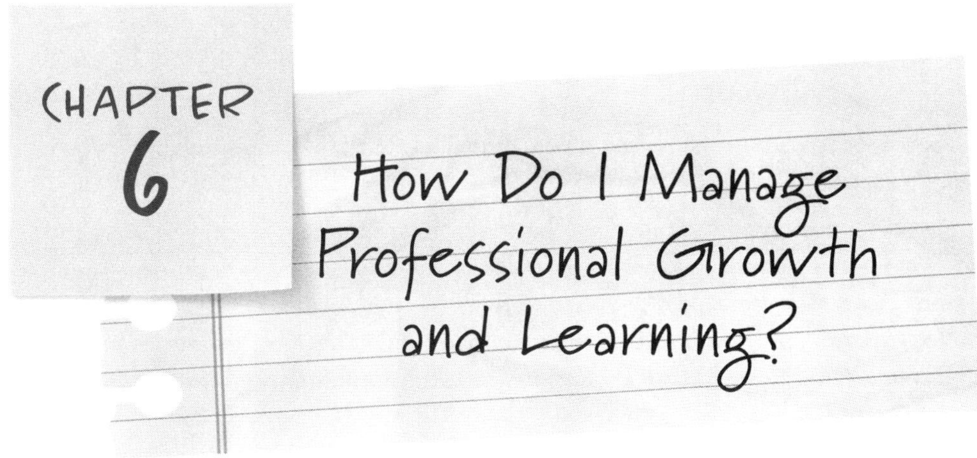

Learning is what it is all about—learning for all students, for all staff, and for yourself. No one will ever know it all. There is always new research that can support you to be the best educator you can be. Meeting the needs of every student is vital and complex work. When doing it well, principals, assistant principals, and teachers are lifelong learners. Professional learning and growth are essential for creating learning experiences that are equitable for all students. Sitting in your office while staff participate in a professional learning experience in the library does not convey what you want to model for students *or* staff.

In addition to focusing on your own professional growth, you must support your staff's professional growth. Your commitment to high-quality professional learning is the best route for ensuring every student has high-quality instruction (Darling-Hammond, Wechsler, Levin, Leung-Gagné, & Tozer, 2022).

Focus on Your Professional Growth

Your professional growth is pivotal, and research from Linda Darling-Hammond and colleagues (2022) supports this: "Studies have consistently found that principals participating in comprehensive professional development programs with the features of high-quality professional learning report increases in their understanding of leadership and, where studied, improvements in their leadership practices" (p. 23).

Take the following into consideration as you begin planning your professional learning.

- Start small. See what your district's policy and standards are in relation to principal professional growth.
- Pursue information about instructional leadership, change management, leadership development, school culture creation, and how to meet diverse student needs.
- Seek out peer support.

- Create a flexible growth plan on which you regularly reflect, revise, and plan next steps.

As you plan, consult the reproducible "Principal Reflection and Growth Assessment Tool" (page 88).

Just as teachers support students in having a growth mindset—and you do the same with staff—remember to also apply that belief to yourself. You're a new principal, and the learning curve will be steep, but you're working on it and will get there! Once you start to feel comfortable, it's important to stay curious and continue growing. As you grow, you model for staff, build your professional network, and improve through reflection.

Have a Growth Mindset

Just as you support students' growth mindsets, you will support that in your staff and yourself. You can develop your administrative skills through hard work, ongoing learning and development, high-impact strategies, and feedback from others (Dweck, 2016). We believe high-quality feedback is the best strategy for professional growth.

Though many principals report receiving feedback that is ambiguous, inconsistent, or unrelated to their day-to-day jobs, high-quality feedback is one of the most effective instruments for professional development. A coaching attitude about supervision helps you transform the feedback you get into a consistent, introspective, and practical component of leadership development. Consistent and timely reciprocal feedback discussions that focus on best leadership practices are proven to positively impact principal growth; this feedback cycle is collaborative and promotes ongoing learning (EduSolve, n.d.).

Remember, learners with a growth mindset tend to achieve more than those with a more fixed mindset, those who believe their talents are innate gifts that they cannot influence (Dweck, 2016). It applies to learning multiplication tables, and it applies to learning how to use data to effectively lead a building full of staff and students. In our work with principals, those with a growth mindset practiced humility, were open to listening to others' ideas and experiences, and were open to feedback about their work. It's important to put your energy into learning instead of appearing as if you know everything. No one does, and that's OK.

Be the Model

We've said it before and we're saying it again: Be the model for your staff and students. But where do you start with your own professional growth now that you are the school leader? Your province or state may have professional standards that school leaders need to adhere to. This is a good place to begin. Familiarize yourself with the standard and determine which area you need to focus on.

It's not uncommon to choose a standard that focuses on the managerial aspects of this new role. We do not recommend this. Believe it or not, managing people will not be the key to your success as a school leader. Standards that focus on school culture, vision and mission, instructional leadership, and so on will provide you with a deeper understanding of the work you need to do and the knowledge and skills required to move your school forward. Research indicates that "leading instruction, managing change, developing people, shaping a positive school culture, and meeting the needs of diverse learners" are most important for principal preparation (Darling-Hammond et al., 2022, p. 75).

If your province or state does not have a standard, it may be worthwhile to investigate some from a similar province or state. Many speak to the same knowledge, skills, and attributes. Connect with other school leaders for support and coaching (Darling-Hammond et al., 2022). In our experience, school leaders want to help one another; they just need to be asked. Those peer relationships are just one part of effective professional learning: "Some research has found that professional learning opportunities for principals, such as high-quality preparation programs, ongoing training, peer networks, and coaching support, can build leadership capacity and reduce principal turnover" (Levin & Bradley, 2020, p. 19).

Tips to Thrive

At school, model a love of learning by sharing articles, talking about books you've read, reflecting aloud about workshops or other events, and debriefing after participating in professional learning experiences alongside staff. For example, you might make copies of professional journal articles that pertain to your goals and put them in staff mailboxes. Ask staff to come to your next staff meeting prepared to discuss their thoughts regarding the article.

Similar to your professional growth goals, your state or province may have a format they want you to use for planning. If that's the case, they will also have a policy or an administrative procedure that outlines your growth planning. However, if this is not the case, several formats and templates are available online—just search the topic. The reproducible "Professional Growth Plan" (page 91) covers what many districts require. The main thing is to ensure you choose a goal that allows you to have a positive impact on the work you're doing in your school. Revisit it regularly.

Don't overwhelm yourself. Research, begin planning, seek out advice from your network of colleagues, and revise before moving forward. Most reputable professional organizations have online and print resources and host professional learning sessions throughout the year.

Build Your Professional Network

A professional network of colleagues who you feel comfortable learning with and from will make a big difference (Levin & Bradley, 2020). Their varying experiences can support you in your professional learning, and they can provide advice on the complex work of school leadership. This is the collaboration you hopefully used to receive as a teacher. Now, you must reach outside your school to do that collaborating.

There are many ways you can build your network. Here are just a few examples.

- Join your provincial or state professional association.
- Attend conferences and workshops.
- Listen to, read, and reflect on blogs, podcasts, and other resources.
- Socialize with other leaders and participate in special projects and events.
- Present at conferences and meetings.

When you socialize, you will meet fellow administrators at district professional learning sessions and meetings. Once you make a few connections, you can further develop your relationship through phone calls, going for coffee, and the like. We worked with a group of principals who attended a monthly breakfast meeting prior to our administrative learning sessions.

Your cadre can share successes and growth opportunities regarding professional learning implementation, resources, and learning about best practices across schools. The relationships you build and maintain for years can have a direct positive impact on your future success as a leader.

Tips to Thrive

The quality of the relationships you build in your network is much more important than the number of relationships.

Improve Through Reflection

An ongoing reflective process supports a deeper understanding of your professional identity and the impact of your actions on students and staff. Reflecting deliberately fosters "engagement in learning and increased learning outcomes" (Ribeiro et al., 2019). To learn and get better, we must reflect. Reflection plays a key role in professional learning by encouraging individuals to critically examine their practices, beliefs, and assumptions (Anderson & Rincón-Gallardo, 2021). Consider keeping a journal of your daily activities. At the end of each day, read it, reflect on your work, and determine the impact on teacher and student growth.

Here are some key points to consider about the significance of reflection in professional learning you will undertake with your staff.

- Reflection encourages you and your teachers to question your long-held beliefs and assumptions. By identifying and addressing these assumptions, you and your teachers can embrace more inclusive, effective, and equitable practices.

- Continuous reflection creates a feedback loop where you and your teachers can assess the outcomes of your actions. This iterative process allows for adjustments in teaching, which lead to better student outcomes.
- Professional learning communities that value collaborative reflection can deepen the learning experience. Sharing insights and constructive feedback with peers fosters a supportive environment and promotes collective growth.

Allocate dedicated time for your own reflection in professional learning opportunities—your own and those provided by a third party. Structured time during workshops, collaborative meetings, or self-directed reflection exercises should be intentionally planned.

One colleague commented that having a student teacher was one of the best professional learning gifts they had ever received because the student asked "why" a lot. Why did you introduce your lesson this way? Why are you teaching this? This student teacher taught our colleague about the power of reflection. Our colleague had to think about how they were teaching, planning, and assessing, and if the answer to the "why" wasn't, "It is helping students to learn and be successful," then it needed to be removed from their pedagogy.

Tips to Thrive

Self-care is very individual; it doesn't look the same for everyone. Determine what you need in your routine to ensure you are taking good care of yourself. Some helpful strategies follow.

- Book a lunch date with a student, staff member, or class (so you actually sit down to eat your meal).
- Spend time walking outside of the school building daily, even if just for ten minutes.
- Set up a daily exercise routine, such as walking, yoga, or a morning run.
- Spend time with your friends or family every week.
- Participate in a community program or service project.
- Pursue a creative class like painting or guitar.

Support Your Staff's Professional Growth

It may help you to think of your staff as being your new class. Just like a class of students, they have strengths and areas for growth. In fact, "professional and personal growth are factors in teachers' positive interactions, and it improves their dedication to their employment" (Lim, 2021, p. 21). It is your task to get to know them, help them plan, and support them through their learning to be their best for students. This includes helping them fulfill their professional learning needs.

As we discussed in chapter 5, the more you are in classrooms supervising and providing feedback, the better able you are to support and provide professional learning experiences for your staff. One of the most important things for you to remember is that professional learning should result in greater learning for all students. While you are engaging in classroom walkthroughs and having feedback conversations with teachers, you are also gathering data about individual and school-based professional learning needs. Decisions regarding professional learning foci are much more compelling if they are linked to data.

You can enhance staff professional growth with the following strategies: collaborating on professional growth plans, supporting high-quality professional learning experiences, using data to target the learning focus, reinforcing the importance of collaboration, and including other stakeholders in professional learning.

Collaborate on Professional Growth Plans

Professional growth planning for individual teachers can be complex. The main desired outcome is positively impacting student success, but teachers need to feel ownership of their plans. Those plans should always include goals that will make a difference for the students in their care.

It can be beneficial to schedule individual meetings at least three times—(1) beginning of the year, (2) mid-year, and (3) year's end—with your staff to go over their growth plans. This helps you become familiar with how you can support each staff member and what you should look for during classroom visits. The end-of-the-year meeting allows for reflection on successes and next steps. This brings a measure of accountability to their individual plans and shows that you are committed to supporting them in growing professionally. These meetings also emphasize that this growth plan is a living document and not something to complete at the beginning of the year and then file away.

Figure 6.1 has questions you may want to use to frame these discussions.

What is your focus for your professional growth this year?
Walk me through your plan. What data have you used to determine your focus?
How can I help you? How can your colleagues help you?
What resources will you need?
How can you access these resources?
What will you accept as evidence that you are reaching your goals?

Figure 6.1: Professional growth plan questions.

Visit ***go.SolutionTree.com/leadership*** *for a free reproducible version of this figure.*

Many school authorities have specific formats for plans like this, and you can find numerous examples of the process online by searching for professional growth plan examples for teachers. Consider allowing staff to choose the format for their plan. One principal we knew had a staff member who created her growth plan using a cereal box.

Her learning goal was presented on the front of the box. One side of the box listed the strategies she would use to achieve her goal, and the other side of the box detailed the resources she would be using. The back of the box outlined the evidence she would be looking for to determine whether she was moving toward achieving her goal. Inside the box was a journal that she planned on using to keep data, reflections, and artifacts.

As psychology professor Viviane Robinson (2023) contends, one of the biggest hurdles in professional learning is the issue of capability. For teachers to grow professionally, they have to focus on a gap between their current and required levels of capability. Ensure that staff learning goals are ambitious and based on data. Data provides a clear picture of where you need to support both individual and whole-staff professional learning. That data can come from anywhere: regular classroom walkthroughs; classroom, school, and provincial or state assessments; teachers' professional judgment (what they know about their students' academic and social-emotional needs); and more.

For example, assume that one of your teachers is concerned they don't have enough time in their day to teach anything but language arts and some mathematics. This might confuse you if you've observed them teaching other subjects several times. You might have a discussion or visit the class to see what has changed. After visiting, perhaps you discover that they are trying to employ all the strategies they learned at a professional learning conference instead of choosing one or two to try for an extended period. After school, you could meet with the teacher and talk about the lessons, reflecting on the focus of each lesson. Together, you could look at which strategy was having the greatest impact on students.

Support High-Quality Professional Learning Experiences

High-quality professional learning provides powerful opportunities to influence the quality of teaching and learning within your school. High-quality professional learning can raise teachers' self-efficacy, improve teacher practice and collaboration, and increase student capabilities (Darling-Hammond et al., 2017).

A great deal of research has been done regarding effective professional learning. In an action research study that we conducted with partners from the University of Calgary, we determined that effective professional learning must have the following characteristics (Thomas et al., 2021).

- Be sustained over time with a consistent focus.
- Use collaborative learning approaches.
- Assess growth through reflection and feedback.
- Use action research to support continuous improvement.

Additionally, research includes these requirements for effective professional learning (Campbell, Osmond-Johnson, Faubert, Zeichner, & Hobbs-Johnson, 2017; Darling-Hammond et al., 2017; Robinson, 2023).

- Responds to evidence of specific student and teacher learning needs

- Offers rich evidence-based content that is based on sound research and has been rigorously evaluated (not just this year's newest trend)
- Is personal and responsive

This brings us back to the idea that your staff are your class. Consequently, when you are planning schoolwide professional learning sessions, it's crucial to know your learners, their strengths in the areas you are focusing on, and their needs. There can be whole-class sessions, but scaffold and enrich the content to meet the needs of all your learners (just like teachers do in their classrooms).

Figure 6.2 is a tool you can keep on hand as guidance as you plan.

1. **Welcome:** Greet everyone and review your norms. As discussed in chapter 3, it is important that you have a set of norms in place every time your staff are working together.
2. **Group development:** Provide an activity that focuses on deepening staff relationships. Emphasize that you are all in this together. You might be surprised how little your staff knows about one another, especially in relation to their practice.
3. **The reason:** Review why you're learning. Shan's grandfather, who was a high school principal, always said, "Repeat the sounding joy!" We cannot overemphasize the why of our work. It anchors everything we do.
4. **Learn:** Depending on your topic, you might be the one leading this portion of your session, or it may be one of your staff or an outside speaker. The important thing to remember is whomever is conducting the learning portion needs to be seen as an expert in the topic. In addition, each of our school-based professional learning experiences had a time where we could provide differentiation for our learners.
5. **Wrap up:** We always ensured staff had the opportunity to reflect on their learning experiences and plan for their own individual next steps in relation to their learning. We also had them share their next steps with a learning partner to add some accountability to this process.

Figure 6.2: Basic guide for planning schoolwide professional learning.
Visit ***go.SolutionTree.com/leadership*** *for a free reproducible version of this figure.*

Use Data to Target the Learning Focus

Data is a collection of information, including numbers, words, and observations, that's organized in a way that helps educators make informed decisions. Using data is key to informing both the goals for whole-school and individual professional learning. Without data, you are guessing what you need to do. Data—such as state or provincial test results, district assessments, school-based assessments, teachers' professional judgment, and behavioral, attendance, and student satisfaction data (looking for engagement, for instance)—informs your decisions regarding professional learning focus areas for both yourself and your staff. Depending on what data you collect and for what purpose, you may be the only one who looks at it. On the other hand, a teacher team or the whole staff may use a data set.

For data to inform professional learning, it is important to share all data in easily understood and actionable ways. For example, when tasked with improving third-grade literacy rates, the whole third-grade learning team examines the data and plans next steps. Rather than placing attention on the scores, the data analysis focuses staff on what everyone will do; it places the conversation squarely on student success. Take behavior data during times of transition—an area where undesirable behaviors more commonly occur—as another example. Staff will determine strategies they can use to ensure students who struggle during these times learn how to manage themselves. When reviewing data with your staff, the main objective is to determine where you are, where you want to be, and what key barriers and growth opportunities lie between the two.

It's important to always remember that you are using data to *improve*, not to *prove*. Staff's first instinct when looking at data might be to say, "See? We told you so. This group of students lacks basic numeracy skills." This is not a productive mindset about data. However, we *do* want to look at the data and say, "These students need support with basic numeracy skills. What can we do?"

We have observed many principals using a growth-focused process to examine a data set. One such principal, along with her staff, developed a school-based survey for students to see what they felt would make school and their classes more engaging. From this survey, she and her staff could see that the students wanted more active learning and opportunities to collaborate with one another. One staff member had positive responses in relation to engagement and willingly took the lead in sharing strategies with their colleagues.

This principal and a team of staff planned for their professional learning to focus on strategies and structures that increased student engagement. At key times during the school year, they touched back in with their students to see if the learning they were doing in relation to engagement was having an impact at the classroom and school levels. Teachers also kept track of the strategies and structures they were using in their classrooms.

During instructional walkthroughs, this principal also looked for these strategies and structures and would debrief with staff regarding their impact. The academic and satisfaction data for this school continued to reflect that this work was having a positive impact on student engagement and academic success at all levels. Staff could easily share the strategies and structures that were causing this positive result and together determine the next steps in their professional learning journeys.

Reinforce the Importance of Collaboration

Some teachers want to go to their classroom, close the door, and teach. However, educators need to work together to meet the needs of all students. Collaboration is the context in which people with different strengths and perspectives come together to achieve a shared goal. In this case, learning is the goal, and collaboration improves that. But there are other benefits as well: "Not only does collaboration improve teachers' professional knowledge and experience, but also it significantly improves student learning and achievement" (Ostovar-Nameghi & Sheikhahmadi, 2016, p. 199). Through collaboration, teams can break down silos, share knowledge, and unlock new ideas, resulting in something greater than what anyone could accomplish alone.

It's important to remember that just saying "let's collaborate" doesn't make true collaboration happen. In chapters 4 and 5, we discussed what conditions need to be in place for true collaboration to happen. In a collaborative professional learning environment, staff strengths and growth opportunities are openly shared, and learning and growth are celebrated.

Consider this example: We worked with a team of principals who openly shared the work that was positively impacting learning for all students, but they were also very open about where they were struggling. As the district became more collaborative, principals opened the doors of their schools to their colleagues for visits, observations, questions, and reciprocal learning. This is what it looks like in a school that is collaborative—teachers have an open-door policy, and they openly share and question each other's practice. In one school where we worked, the principal and assistant principal would release their teachers (by teaching their classes) so they could visit each other's classrooms to observe lessons and learn success strategies.

Additionally, as we will discuss in chapter 7, sharing leadership and the work also supports collaboration. You do not have to plan all of your school's professional learning on your own. Having a committee or a team of staff involved supports teacher efficiency and engagement.

Include Other Stakeholders in Professional Learning

During our time in education, we have all faced the questions that come from stakeholders regarding the amount of professional learning that is provided to leaders and staff. These are questions like, Why do they have so many days off? Don't they already know how to teach? Is this professional development day really making a difference for my child?

How you respond to these questions indicates how much you value professional learning. Provide stakeholders with an in-depth understanding of why professional learning is so important. It's important to provide a few brief but explicit reasons so they can see why professional learning is critical. For example, having a single-page flyer with data and cited research with four bullet points can be a good way to communicate. You can do this through your newsletter, meetings, and open houses. You also can provide professional learning opportunities for families and other community members that mirror your and your staff's learning. For example, each teacher could design a mathematics lesson for caregivers and provide students with tips on how the adults at home can support this lesson.

Providing professional learning for other stakeholders is another way to support equity for all students. For example, invite families to learn about strategies they can use at home to support their child's learning. You can host learning evenings for community partners, where you and other staff reveal the work you do and share learning that the broader community can enact in their environments.

This also engages families and the broader community, which is discussed further on pages 24 and 32. Family learning sessions are opportunities for families to learn about and observe the learning activities their children are engaged in. These sessions also build engagement; you can hold one per quarter and break it into grade or subject area throughout the year. You can ask teachers and students to offer different stations for families to participate in. On one such night, we worked with a school focused on literacy. Parents, grandparents, siblings, and guardians for first grade watched a student and teacher model an alphabet game that visitors then played with their child. In a fifth-grade classroom, students and the teacher reviewed the components of a paragraph, and attendees practiced the same lesson with a partner.

Final Thoughts: It's All About Learning

Professional learning is key to achieving success for all students and closing the gap. Through the data you have available, you will determine the growth goals for your school and the professional learning needs for yourself, the whole staff, and stakeholders. Professional growth plans will guide this work and need to be living documents that are shared, discussed, and celebrated.

Planning professional development is a collaborative process, and you can bring colleagues on board to support you with this work. When you look at your staff like they are your class, you can plan for them like you would a group of students and ensure that their learning is engaging, differentiated, and has a positive impact on student success.

Principal Reflection and Growth Assessment Tool

This reflection and growth assessment tool can support you in your current practices, goals, and growth in key areas of school leadership.

Self-Reflection

For each of the following aspects, please reflect on the following. Then answer the overall reflection questions and plan your next steps.

- Where I have been (experiences, challenges, and learning)
- Where I am (current practices, strengths, and realities)
- Where I hope to be (vision, goals, and next steps)

Relationships
Where I have been:
Where I am:
Where I hope to be:
Communication
Where I have been:
Where I am:
Where I hope to be:
Culture Creation
Where I have been:
Where I am:
Where I hope to be:

Instructional Leadership
Where I have been:
Where I am:
Where I hope to be:
Professional Growth
Where I have been:
Where I am:
Where I hope to be:
Leadership Building in Others
Where I have been:
Where I am:
Where I hope to be:
Additional Duties
Where I have been:
Where I am:
Where I hope to be:

page 2 of 3

Overall Reflection

What has been my biggest success as a school leader so far?
What has been my biggest challenge or growth area?
What is my top leadership priority for the upcoming school year?

Action Planning

Next steps for the next three months:
Long-term goals (one to three years):
Necessary support and resources:

Professional Growth Plan

Name:
School Year:
School:
Goal Description (*What leadership knowledge or skills do you need to further develop to impact your work as a school leader?*)
Leadership Competency or Standard (*Which teaching competencies or standards are linked to your goal?*)
Strategies (*What learning activities will you use to meet your goal?*) ☐ ☐ ☐
Timeline (*When will these activities take place?*) ☐ ☐ ☐
Resources (*What tools and supports do you need?*) ☐ ☐ ☐
Progress Indicators (*How will you measure your growth? What shows evidence of success? How will you know when you've achieved your goal?*)
Reflection and Next Steps (*During the school year, regularly reflect on your progress and growth in relation to your goal. Briefly summarize any key learnings, successes, and further opportunities for growth. What will you do next to continue your learning?*)

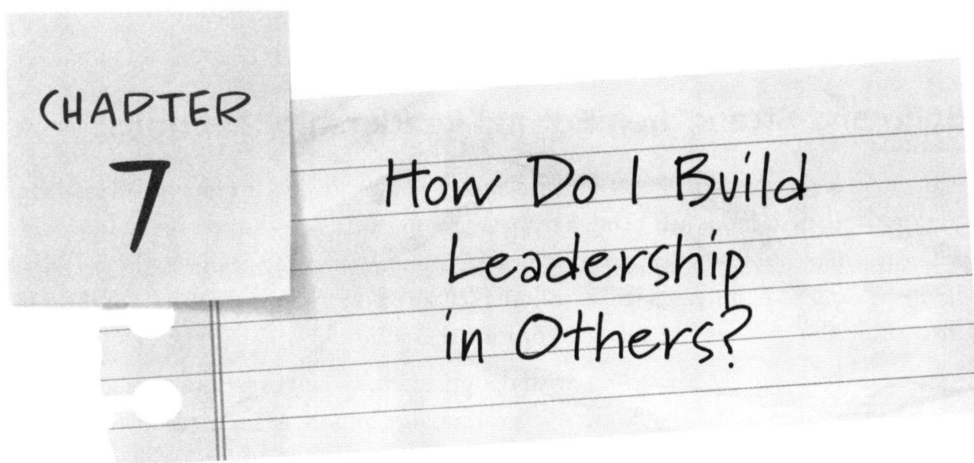

The role of the principal has become more complex, and the responsibilities and accountability of the position have increased the need for others to share the load: "Leadership encompasses a set of functions that may be performed by many different persons in different roles throughout a school" (Leithwood & Riehl, 2003, p. 2). Leading a school is all-encompassing, so it's important for you, as the principal, to engage with your staff, families, and students and build their capacity to lead where possible.

Shared leadership roles are often referred to as *collective* or *distributed leadership*. Distributed leadership is a partnership where teacher leaders and others get the necessary support to level up their leadership know-how (New Leaders, n.d.). It benefits everyone. In addition to supporting the principal, research shows that distributed leadership helps build the school's capacity to hone teachers' leadership skills. The Ontario Leadership Strategy under the Ontario Ministry of Education (2012) identifies three benefits of developing people: "[1] stimulating growth in the professional capacities of staff; [2] modeling of the school's values and practices; and [3] building trusting relationships with and among staff, students, and parents" (p. 17). Additional research supports these findings:

> Results point toward the significance of distributed leadership for other aspects of school culture, such as professional collaboration and self-efficacy, positively associated with teacher job satisfaction and student achievement. Schools that are structured to increase leadership opportunities for teachers hold great potential in providing positive work environments conducive to student achievement in the most disadvantaged schools. (Torres, 2019)

Leadership can be at the classroom level, at a whole-school level, or as a support mechanism through parent councils. As principal, you identify potential leaders, nurture them, and mentor them in their leadership skills. Building and strengthening formal and informal leadership positions is work, but the final result benefits those leaders, the students, and you. You will lead by example.

Build and Strengthen Formal Leadership Positions

The roles and responsibilities of the principal have expanded to the level that leadership needs to be shared. From just being a manager to now being an instructional leader with the added responsibilities of managing resources and facilitating budgets, the principal needs the support of other leaders within the school to meet the complexities of the role. These leadership roles can be informal or formal.

Formalized leadership roles come with designated titles and organizational authority. In education, these formalized leadership positions are important for a variety of reasons, as they provide the necessary support for students and teachers. Some examples of formal leadership positions include assistant principal, acting administrator, and department heads, as outlined in the following sections.

Assistant Principal

You may be in a school where an assistant principal has been assigned, or you may have the opportunity to choose your own. Either way, count yourself lucky to be in this position. You have a colleague with whom you can share ideas, discuss scenarios, and make collaborative decisions—and this person will fill in for you when you're not on campus. Modeling strong leadership skills is necessary because you are mentoring the assistant principal whose role will depend on what you, as principal, decide you want to "share or delegate" (Winemiller, 2019).

Lots of administration teams will share duties and responsibilities, and some will divvy up what needs to be done. Many times, assistant principals get assigned menial tasks that don't help them develop their leadership skills, such as handling student discipline. While this is necessary in the day-to-day running of a school, it doesn't necessarily require the skills of a strong leader.

Avoid delegating only mundane or low-responsibility tasks that do not challenge your colleague. Give your assistant principal responsibilities that involve the educational side of the work, such as leading a report card committee or taking the lead in providing professional learning opportunities for staff. Remember, you are supporting the assistant principal in developing the skills necessary to become a principal.

An assistant principalship is the training ground for a principalship, so ensure they are learning what they need. This can be difficult as you both learn your roles in this new partnership. Just as you are the facilitator and contact point for teachers' continual learning and improvement, you are also those things for your assistant principal. Through informal and formal observations and discussions, your assistant principal will discover their strengths and growth opportunities.

Some districts have principals or district staff complete assistant principal evaluations. Most school districts have competencies or standards that their administrators must attain. When you are hired for this role, sharing these competencies and standards is part of the onboarding process. You can share some duties with the assistant principal and even let them take the lead on various responsibilities but always check in and support them. Trust that your assistant principal will do the work but check in to ensure that what you expect is being done. It is your work to support them in learning and achieving these competencies.

Acting Administrator

Many schools have a designated acting administrator when the principal and any assistant principals are required to be out of the school for a day or longer. In this case, the principal chooses one or more teachers to assume the role of acting administrator. Generally, a substitute teacher covers the individual's teaching tasks so the acting administrator can attend to any matters that might arise. Some schools alternate the position between a few teachers on staff, while some just have one designated per year.

When choosing an acting administrator, consider the following information, which you will have gained through class visits, staff meeting behaviors, and position interviews.

- Do their colleagues respect them? (Do their colleagues go to them for advice? Do their colleagues often choose them to lead discussions?)
- Can they make reasonable decisions? (Would you go to them for advice? Can you rely on them to weigh all factors when making decisions? Do you observe them using fair and restorative behavior practices with students?)
- Are they comfortable taking action? (Are they often the staff member who brings things to your attention? Are their classroom practices innovative?)

You can have individuals apply for the designation, and you can conduct interviews to determine who is best suited for the role. The reproducibles "Acting Administrator Application" (page 104) and "Acting Administrator Interview" (page 105) are provided.

Once you choose your acting administrator, be clear with them about what their responsibilities are and aren't. Typically, they deal only with emergent matters, such as student accidents or injuries, severe weather protocols, and student discipline. Any other items can and should be left for you.

Similar to substitute teacher files that teachers prepare, you should have one for the acting administrator. Leave a copy of this document with your administrative assistant or put it in an accessible spot in your office. In it, outline any procedures they might not be as familiar with, such as the following.

- Maintenance procedures
- More in-depth behavior procedures
- Behavior contracts developed for specific students
- Transportation call-out lists
- List of staff whose classes they could cover during the day if time allows (optional)
- Individual students who require extra support (optional)

One huge benefit of having others in this position is that they'll most likely develop an especially healthy respect for the work you do each day after having to fill in for you.

Department Heads

Many high schools and middle schools have department heads for subject areas like mathematics, sciences, humanities, athletics, and arts. Having a teacher serve as a department head can be an excellent opportunity for them to develop and refine their leadership skills while still teaching in the classroom.

Develop a description that outlines the specific duties and responsibilities of the department head position, have interested teachers apply, and then interview for the position. The reproducibles "Department Head Application" (page 108) and "Department Head Interview" (page 109) are provided. For the most part, they may be responsible for leading discussions of a curricular nature and possibly leading the creation of unit and final common exams for their department.

You will work closely with and support these individuals as the principal. Talk through the aspects of this role, provide the department's budget template, and discuss examples of how previous department heads have managed it. (You will review those details prior to the meeting.) Develop a meeting agenda for the department together. After, debrief how the meeting went and note any priority areas for purchases, identified professional needs, and so on.

Build and Strengthen Informal Leadership Positions

Informal leadership is an extremely important means of complementing formal leadership. These individuals hold no organizational power but impact the overall learning environment and school community. Informal leaders influence your school's culture and can be teachers, teacher leaders, students, parents, or guardians. Building relationships with all stakeholders (page 15) is directly related to your ability to build and strengthen these roles.

Teacher Leaders

Teacher leaders are educators who are known to go beyond the traditional role of classroom instruction to influence and improve educational practices at the school's various levels. Teacher leaders enhance student learning outcomes and their fellow teachers' professional work by contributing to their schools. Teacher leaders support principals in aspects of their work where they are not as strong and help improve relationships throughout the school by creating a trusting environment.

Some people have natural leadership skills, suggesting ideas, organizing events, or working as part of a team to move a project forward. These people are a great starting point—work with them to hone their skills. As you interact with your teachers, you will notice good teacher leader candidates do the following.

- Step up to volunteer.
- Actively engage in the learning process (such as incorporating new instructional strategies).
- Quietly lead by example.

These individuals may need you to encourage them to step into leadership. For example, you might ask, "Have you ever considered leading our literacy team?" or "You have a real strength in classroom management. Would you consider having colleagues visit your classroom?" With your support, they will help lead the school in positive ways.

How do you support them as they develop their leadership skills? You can do this through a variety of means, including sharing best practices at staff meetings, hosting meetings, helping build strong networks, and setting up opportunities to lead.

Share Best Practices at Staff Meetings

You can have these teacher leaders share their practices at a staff meeting, or you can create opportunities for other teachers to do a classroom visit to watch the teacher in action. You can support this by covering the other teacher's class or bringing in a substitute teacher so teachers are freed up to visit each other's classrooms. If other teachers can learn from their peers through professional development, a strong pedagogical teacher can share what effective approaches they use in their classrooms. Maybe they have been working on collaborative learning strategies that have increased student engagement, and as a result, students are developing a better understanding of concepts they're learning.

Host Meetings

Ask those who are interested to sign up to host staff meetings about something they are having success with in their classrooms. Fellow teachers take the first few minutes to complete a classroom walkabout and ask questions. During the second year, if there are teachers who haven't signed up, you can specifically ask them to consider hosting.

Help Build Strong Networks

Getting colleagues together to work on instructional strategies creates a network for them. Once teachers know that they can be vulnerable with their colleagues, they will be more likely to share their struggles as well as their successes. Having strong networks through professional relationships fosters conversations that can enhance teaching skills and students' learning. The more opportunities teachers have to discuss their craft, the better the teaching and learning will be. When teachers hear about others' successes, they are generally more willing to try something new.

Set Up Opportunities to Lead

Staff members may need more support from you if they lack the confidence to lead, and you can set up specific opportunities for them. They could take a leadership role within certain committees, such as a graduation committee or a staff social committee. Your support would include ensuring that they know the purpose of the committee and what the expectations are. For example, say you have identified a teacher who is using a new instructional strategy that is working well for students. You can approach them to lead your next professional development session where they share this strategy. Together, you meet to set up the agenda. During the professional development session, you introduce them and allow them to lead. You are still there to support them, but having spent time preparing the session with them, you are confident they can do it on their own.

Tips to Thrive

Use a think-aloud strategy when talking through the steps in your decision-making processes and the work you do. Just as teachers use this in the classroom, it can work with adults. For example, you might say aloud during a staff meeting, "I was thinking that we would hold our spring concert in the afternoon this year. However, when I asked for your thoughts, you said that would make it hard for caregivers who work, so I went back to the drawing board. There are a lot of evening events during the month that we host our spring concert, and attendance is usually low. But the evening does not take away from the review time you need for the upcoming assessments. What if we record the concert and put it on our school YouTube channel?"

Parent and Guardian Leadership

Families have lots of caregivers who play significant roles in students' lives: co-parents, grandparents, aunts and uncles, siblings, foster or adoptive parents, and other recognized guardians. These people are a child's first teacher and have a wealth of knowledge about their child and the whole community. You benefit from this knowledge when you create relationships with them (page 24) and foster leadership in this group. This leadership opportunity can help adults become the go-to people in their neighborhoods for those who want to understand what is happening in your school (for example, when someone wants to know what your school goals are and the progress you are making toward them). They can support the work you're doing.

A parent or guardian might tap into leadership around the following.

- Advising the principal
- Communicating with the broader community

For any parent or guardian leadership opportunity, the adults must truly have a voice in the decisions that are made, or it will be tokenism. That is not advocacy. Families, just like staff and students, need mentorship and encouragement in their leadership journeys. If a family needs support beyond your school's capacity, point them to a community support that addresses their needs. For example, a family who is going through a divorce might need emotional support, so they look for a counselor to assist.

Advise the Principal

Schools usually have parent leadership groups called parent-teacher associations, school councils, or similar titles. These groups provide advice and support to the principal. They work with principals to effectively enhance learning for all students. They provide a means for members of the school community to consult with and provide advice to the principal.

The parent council may be asked to advise about the following topics.

- The school's overall mission, philosophy, policies, and goals
- The school's improvement plan
- The school's budget

These topics would be brought to a parent council meeting. You can employ the strategies, such as around the world, that you use during staff meetings when going over these topics. One person can share ideas about one topic, and subsequent groups can add to the prior group's thoughts.

Tips to Thrive

We have seen families lead open houses, organize and coach reading volunteers, run events at sports day, and more. Don't worry if you can't come up with a project for them to lead—they will!

Communicate With the Broader Community

Parents and guardians can be the information pipeline to the broader community. They can be helpful in sharing information regarding programs offered in the school, extracurricular activities, upcoming events, and school achievement results. Keep them informed and craft their messaging. For example, say you have finished a mid-year literacy assessment focused on comprehension, and the scores demonstrate growth. You can work with your family leadership group to write a consistent message regarding the information. If families have a clear understanding of the work you're doing, they will be your advocates in your parking lot and beyond. By the school administering questionnaires and formal discussions, families can discover the community's views.

Just as you do with staff, you need to check in and monitor these leadership opportunities. And, of course, be sure to publicly recognize these family leaders as often as possible. They'll appreciate the recognition—especially if their own children see the impact of their leadership.

Student Leadership

One of the least-used resources in our schools is the students. The relationships and connection you have with them in your role as principal will be a huge part of your success or failure. Even students as young as four years old have something to say about what they need from their school.

Students need to feel like they belong; they are cared for, safe, and heard; and they have ownership. Students need to feel that what is happening in their school is being done *with* them. You can lessen many behavioral issues that happen in schools by providing leadership opportunities for students. Student leadership significantly influences positive behavioral change (Ahumuza & Kazaara, 2024).

As with anything, hard work and preparation up front reap the rewards. Student leadership opportunities provide students with the skills to do the following (Abbas, Mahjabeen, Ayub, & Iqbal, 2024).

- Take responsibility for oneself, including developing academic and personal independence.
- Take care of their individual workspace, classroom, and school.
- Help each other through the learning process.
- Have a positive mindset.
- Develop a voice.

Having students learn leadership skills not only benefit their development, but it also helps their interactions with others. It helps students learn the importance of watching out for one another, modeling important skills for their fellow students, and promoting ownership and voice in their learning and school. Who knows, maybe some of these students will one day become principals and lead their own schools!

There are many ways in which students can lead in your school: designating leadership groups, establishing a principal advisory group, giving students a voice in school communications, and having students lead new projects. Some of these opportunities lend themselves to certain age groups, but even the youngest students in your school can lead.

Designate Leadership Groups

Many schools have student leadership groups or student councils. Often students are elected to positions for these opportunities. Having specified leadership goals is one way to structure the groups, and students can be responsible for leading a multitude of things around the school, such as the following.

- Reading announcements
- Serving as representatives on a district student voice committee
- Modeling and teaching schoolwide behavior expectations at assemblies and formally in classrooms
- Providing playground activities and teaching games to younger students at recess

You will oversee these forms of student leadership, but that oversight is also an opportunity for teacher leaders to take on more responsibility.

Establish a Principal Advisory Committee

Schools, no matter what their grade-level configuration is, can have a principal advisory committee. Students are invited to meet regularly with the principal to learn about work the principal and staff are planning for the school. Students are provided with opportunities to share their perspectives in relation to these plans.

Depending on the decision or activity, consider asking the group to take these ideas to the larger student population to garner feedback. It is a great opportunity for students to feel valued and for principals to get to know students and their impressions of the school.

Give Students a Voice

Students can partner with the school administration to communicate with other students and bring their perspectives into the decision-making process. They can informally share things they hear students say they want or need and, sometimes, have the larger student population complete surveys to support moving ideas forward for principal and staff consideration. Secondary students may consider a project that improves the school's property for their use or supports the broader community (such as by raking leaves for elderly residents). Elementary students may need recess game equipment or books for their classroom libraries. Students can also lead the morning announcements, assemblies, or presentations to families and community members.

Have Students Lead New Projects

There are many activities and projects that students lead at any given time, such as a sports team, a recycling initiative, or a festival. Students can become captains, emcee events, or lead visitor tours. When students are given the opportunity to plan and have a leadership role in extracurricular activities, school projects, and events, they have ownership and want to promote their school.

Lead by Example

As the principal, your mentorship is essential for developing leadership capacity in others. When you demonstrate strong leadership skills and qualities, you help create future leaders. Remember that staff, students, and families all look to you for leadership.

Developing strong leaders throughout your school begins with leading by example. Ask yourself the following.

- Am I demonstrating what it means to be a leader?
- Do I arrive on time and am I prepared for meetings?
- Do I act on promises I've made?
- Do I provide opportunities for others to share ideas?
- Do I actually listen to those ideas and make decisions based on the data collected?
- Do I follow through on decisions, commitments, and shared ideas?

Creating opportunities for staff to be part of collegial and collaborative decision making is a more informal way to develop leadership skills. Share data with staff so they know what is going on in the school and, therefore, can be part of the solution to the problem. For example, in sharing the budget with staff, it is apparent that more money for resources and professional learning is needed, but one of those areas will have to be reduced. You can have a good discussion and get your staff's opinions on what is more important in supporting student learning. Again, getting their voice is important, but it doesn't always mean that they make the final decision. Ultimately, those decisions are yours to make after considering all the information collected.

Final Thoughts: Be the Leading Leader

The role of the principal has changed significantly, shifting in focus from managing a school to being a leader. Reflecting on your own leadership skills and determining your strengths and growth areas are good places to start. Continuous learning and improvement are part of being a leader. You want to ensure that you are keeping up with the educational research and modeling the leadership skills necessary in leading a school.

With such a huge list of responsibilities that go hand in hand with running a successful school, you need to garner support for the work by sharing the load. Remember that true leaders don't operate solely on their titles, so while formalized positions are nice, you have a wealth of resources on your staff. Always be on the lookout for natural leaders and teachers with strong pedagogical skills who can be mentored to lead in many areas, especially in supporting their colleagues. By involving staff in decision making, you build their capabilities and their trust in you, which benefit the school.

Involving parents, guardians, and students in leadership is also beneficial. Families can be your strongest allies and advocates. Bring them close and work with them on projects that support the work of your school. Help them see and understand, through their leadership, what your vision and purpose are; they will, in turn, help share the narrative you want. Our students are our greatest resource, so tap into their voice and give them opportunities to lead and be involved in decision making. They have so much to offer.

Acting Administrator Application

Follow up on this application with an in-person interview.

Name:
Grade or subject area:
Why are you interested in being our acting administrator?
What leadership skills will you bring to this role?
List two references:
Follow-up interview date and time:

Acting Administrator Interview

Follow these steps.

1. Welcome the teacher and thank them for applying.
2. Explain the purpose of the interview—to assess readiness to step into the role of acting administrator.
3. Briefly outline the responsibilities—leadership, decision making, safeguarding, staff and student well-being, communication with families and community, and crisis management.
4. Ask the included questions, adding or omitting as the context requires.
5. Last, outline next steps in the process.

Name:
Please highlight some of your leadership experience.
You explained in your application why you are interested in being the acting administrator. Tell me more about that.
How would you maintain the school's vision and culture while serving as acting administrator?
A parent approaches you with a serious concern about a teacher. How would you handle it?
There is a conflict between two staff members that is escalating. What steps would you take?
There is a conflict between two students during recess that escalates. What steps would you take?
If an urgent issue arises that you've never dealt with before, what decision-making process would you follow?

page 2 of 3

How would you prioritize student safety and well-being?
How familiar are you with the school's safety procedures?
Acting administrators often manage day-to-day operations. How would you prioritize competing demands?
How would you balance leadership duties with your own teaching (if applicable)?
What strategies would you use to stay organized under pressure?
Do you have any questions?
Is there anything else you would like to share?

Department Head Application

Follow up on this application with an in-person interview.

Name:
Grade or subject area:
Why are you interested in being department head?
What leadership skills do you bring to this role?
What teaching experience and success have you had that support this role?
List two references:
Follow-up interview date and time:

Department Head Interview

Follow these steps.

1. Welcome the teacher and thank them for applying.
2. Explain the purpose of the interview—to assess readiness to step into the role of department head.
3. Briefly outline the responsibilities.
4. Ask the included questions, adding or omitting as the context requires.
5. Last, outline next steps in the process.

Name:
Can you tell us about your teaching experience and any leadership responsibilities you have undertaken?
What excites you about possibly being department head?
What skills and qualities do you have that make you a good fit for this role?
What is your vision for the department over the next three years?
How would you ensure that the curriculum is ambitious, inclusive, and meets all students' needs?
How would you support and mentor less experienced teachers in your department?
What strategies would you use to develop a strong, collaborative team culture?

Can you give an example of how you've used data to improve outcomes in your own teaching?
How would you maintain strong communication in your department?
How would you maintain strong communication between departments?
How would you prioritize the department's budget and resources?
Consider if results in your subject area were to drop significantly one year. How would you respond?
Do you have any questions?
Is there anything else you would like to share?

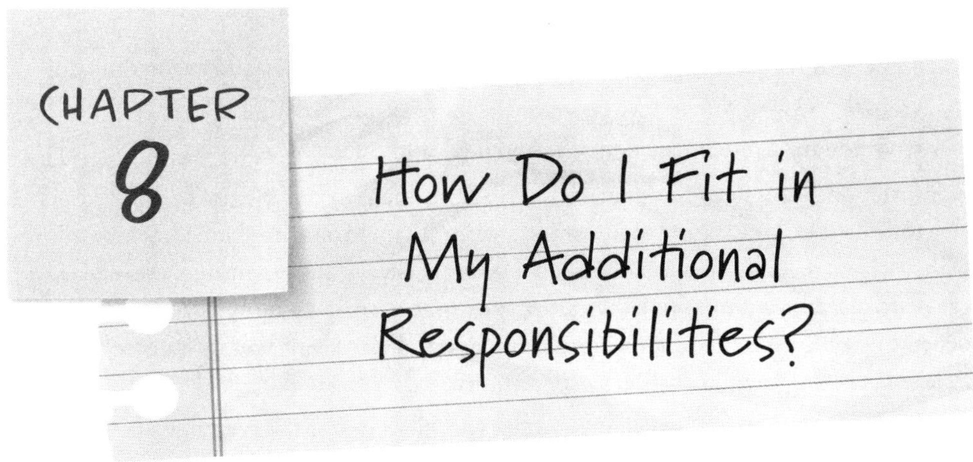

Now that you have a clear understanding of your responsibilities as an instructional leader in a school, there are a plethora of other tasks that need to be done to keep the school running. From budgeting to organizing schedules, the job of the principal is never done. A principal's managerial tasks that support the learning environment ensure that adequate resources are available to all staff and students and that legal policies and frameworks are followed. This chapter provides an overview of numerous complicated tasks—understanding district expectations, acquiring the skills you need, and managing your time and others' time—but we also recommend expert resources you can turn to for more detailed information and guidance.

Understand District Expectations

Districts have many expectations a principal must meet in order to fully lead a school. These directives could be in response to decisions made by education departments, ministries of education, the school board, or the central office. As the principal, be aware of and ensure you are meeting the expectations set for you. These are not limited to but include policies and procedures, budgeting, maintaining the physical environment of the school, and ensuring the health and safety of all in the building.

Policies and Procedures

Every school district has policies and administrative procedures that provide the structures for decision making. These are legal documents. Policies and procedures cover many topics, including the following.

- **Business administration:** Transportation, facility rentals, and fees
- **General administration:** Technology, healthy work sites and schools, and emergency closure
- **Instructional programs and materials:** Specific instructional programs such as French immersion and alternative programs

- **Personnel and employee relations:** Staffing, supervision and evaluation, and staff expectations
- **Students:** Student accidents, attendance, and assessments

Instructional programs and materials specific to their school district and the students are crucial for administrators to be familiar with. It's important to share these procedures with staff at a meeting—especially when a policy relates to programming, curricular and extracurricular programs, or other situations that occur at school. A monthly (or so, depending on context) check on procedures and policies keeps you up to date and able to lead according to your district's expectations.

Often, there are critical policies related to specific times of the year so you can review them in a timely manner. You don't need to be able to cite them verbatim; however, you should know the gist of the policy or procedure or at least know that one exists so you can review it if the situation warrants it. For example, perhaps your school district has a policy for inclement weather. It may stipulate whether buses run at various temperatures and would indicate if schools remain open even if buses don't run. You would refresh that policy in your mind as winter nears, so you can communicate with everyone what happens during inclement weather.

Proms and graduations are examples of discrete events that likely have affiliated policies. That may include what is acceptable for programs and whether staff are able to participate in these events. Because they're on the calendar, you can make a note to refamiliarize yourself with these policies prior.

Tips to Thrive

Many districts will send out notices if a policy or procedure has been updated or changed. Read and bookmark those. It's a good idea to create a list of policies and procedures to review every month.

Finance

Budgeting may not be your strong suit, but it is a key responsibility of the principal. You may work in a division that has site-based budgeting where you are responsible for all aspects of the budget, from determining staffing levels to ensuring there are adequate paper towel reserves in the building. Or maybe you have a small budget where staffing is done at the central office, and you need to manage school resources from substitute teacher hours to professional learning for your staff. Whatever the case, you are a key player in the budgeting process and must be aware of your school's financial status.

Get familiar with the software and ensure that you understand where every dollar is going. Allocating resources—learning supports, textbooks, or ensuring that the bathrooms have adequate supplies—is an important part of leading a school (Superville, 2019).

Ask for help if you need it or if you feel overwhelmed with this aspect of your position. Your district may provide support. Most supply a budget template and have finance staff willing to provide face-to-face or online support. You may have a budget committee, or you may lean on your network of colleagues.

Ask the following questions as you review previous school budgets to see where most of the spending has gone.

- Is there equity in the spending, or is one department using a larger amount of resources?
- Are there areas that can be more effective and efficient?

Physical Environment, Health, and Safety

The principal has the overall responsibility to ensure that the physical building is in working order and is a safe environment for teaching and learning to occur (Mormah, 2023). Yes, you would have custodial staff to clean and perform general maintenance for the building, but you are the overseer.

Through observations, and possibly checklists, check every space in the building to identify any potential hazards to the health and safety of students and staff. Some districts have policies and procedures regarding your school's health and safety. Be aware of these regulations and ensure that the school is physically well maintained.

There are also various drills that need to take place throughout the school year that are designed to prepare you in case of an emergency. Know when these drills occur during the year. Fire drills are mandatory so that you can have all students, staff, and visitors exit the building in a timely manner should a fire occur. Other weather-related drills include those for earthquakes and tornadoes, depending on where you are geographically located. Typically, these are shelter-in-place drills where staff and students stay inside the school as the weather threat is outside.

Other emergency drills that have become more prevalent are related to human threats in the building, such as intruders and weapons. Intruder drills are utilized when a threat is outside the building so students and staff can be kept in the school while regular classes continue. If it's a lockdown, that means there is a threat within the building. Your drill would involve getting all students, staff, and visitors behind locked doors and out of sight of any threat.

It is very important to ensure that all types of threats—from nature or from a person—are considered, and safety plans and precautions are in place. Having drills is essential to ensure that students and adults in the building can move quickly to a safe place. Make sure that you schedule these drills as often as your school district's regulation indicates.

Acquire the Skills You Need

Aside from being a strong instructional leader, as principal, you need a set of skills that will allow you to juggle all the roles and responsibilities you have. Your ability to adapt to the ever-changing situations that occur in your school will be an asset. Being constantly aware of what's happening and when and where you need to intervene are skills that develop more acutely over time (Fox, 2021). Try to be flexible and aware; solve problems as they arise and scan your environment for issues.

Be Flexible

We've talked about having a vision and aligning all decisions to ensure you are working toward your goals. However, it is always healthy to listen to others about what they feel is needed or what could enhance the work that is already being done. Everyone wants time with the principal to share their ideas. So, make the time to meet with and listen to others. This may include students, staff, teachers, families, or community members. The time you need depends on many factors, and you will quickly determine whether you need to meet daily, weekly, or monthly.

Having a fifteen- or thirty-minute meeting will do two things: (1) allow you to continue connecting with your stakeholders by building effective relationships as you listen to what they have to say, and (2) provide you with food for thought about how things are done. This doesn't mean that you must implement the ideas that are shared with you, but it allows you the opportunity to build community while considering the thoughts of others.

It's OK to say things like, "I'll have to look into that," or "I'll take that into consideration." That allows you the time and flexibility to consider plausible ideas. It's also OK to say, "That idea just doesn't align with our learning priorities at this time." Don't let someone believe that their ideas are great if they don't merit any further thought or discussion.

Be Aware

As the principal, you need to be aware of everything that's going on in the school. Being observant will help you identify if your staff are acting professionally and are working together to be the best they can for students. Consider the following.

- What are the staff dynamics?
- Are staff collegial and collaborative?
- Do some staff struggle to interact with others?
- Is there conflict bubbling?

If you see something amiss, deal with it to ensure that the school stays focused on the vision and purpose you have outlined.

The same goes for the student body. Ask yourself the following.

- Are students engaged in their learning?
- Are there bullying problems or acts of violence?
- Do students generally follow expectations?
- Are your school results a good indication of student learning?
- Are some students falling behind?

Monitoring student behavior inside and outside the classroom is essential to getting a solid understanding of the culture. Your observations will provide good data as you examine student dynamics in the school. These may be part of a staff meeting agenda.

Solve Problems

Students and staff may come to you to solve their problems. Instead, you want them to solve their own problems. Instill confidence in your staff that they can deal with student issues in the classroom. Students should only be referred to the office for major infringements. You need to handle more serious behaviors, such as violence, but classroom management remains at the classroom level. You take control away from teachers if you allow them to send their students to you for everything that goes on in the classroom (Linsin, 2014). Your staff need to know that you will support them when dealing with caregivers and with student behaviors; it is an important part of building trust (Samuels, 2019). If the staff member is at fault, address that privately.

The same principle applies to conflicts among staff members. Professional regulations outline what teachers should do if they conflict with a colleague. In most cases, they are expected to speak directly to the individual with whom they have a problem (Muir, 2023). If there's no resolution, they may then bring their conflict to you for guidance.

Don't spend time putting out fires. Make sure that your time is spent in classrooms supporting student learning.

Scan the Environment

Keeping on top of the student and staff dynamics will help you with any potential problems with learning and staff and student interactions. However, you also need to monitor and review processes within the school. Look at how things are handled and determine if these practices need to be continued, improved, or renewed. You could use a stop, start, continue exercise with staff or students.

For example, one of us was a new leader at a school with a beautiful front entry but never saw students going in or out through that entrance. Most staff indicated that not using it was a rule, but they didn't know why. Reviewing this at a staff meeting led to the team agreeing that they wanted students to feel like the school was theirs, and they should be able to use the front entryway. Another example occurred at a school where teachers explained that it took an inordinate amount of time to electronically enter their grades on a weekly basis. On reviewing the process, the principal learned that teachers were first recording all assignment marks into a book and then transferring them to the software on a biweekly or monthly basis. The staff explained that they had to hand in their gradebooks at the end of the year. There was simply a misunderstanding. "Handing in their gradebook" was an outdated way of saying their grades were due.

One elementary school traditionally had morning classes, fifteen minutes for eating lunch, and then twenty minutes for outside recess. A teacher explained that students were so anxious to get outside for recess that they either rushed to eat their food or only ate part of it. The teacher also shared that students needed an activity to settle down when returning from noon recess before class. The staff discussed it and decided they would switch the order on a trial basis because the parent council also believed it was worth trying. In their trial, the students went outside for recess and then ate lunch. The staff found that students were far more ready to eat lunch after having physical activity, and eating provided time to settle down so they were ready to learn when the afternoon classes began. Parents and guardians noticed that their children were eating all their lunch as well. A simple switch allowed a positive change for student learning and classroom management.

Manage Your Time and Others' Time

With so many demands on your time, it's hard some days to know where to begin. Schedule your days and do so using something formal. Set reminders so you'll get a notice if you're busy. Scheduling is critical, especially for classroom visits, since so many things can get in the way of doing your most important work. Using a calendar ensures you access every class throughout a biweekly or monthly time frame.

Schedule a consistent time of day for managing email and paperwork. Ultimately, you can come back to this work later if you are needed elsewhere, but by having it in your calendar, you won't lose sight of significant pieces that need attention. Have a conversation with your administrative assistant so they are aware of what is considered sacred time—being in classrooms—and when you can be interrupted. Having said that, it's important that your staff see you as approachable. The people side of your work is the priority. Preserve school hours as people time; use the hours outside the school day as paper time, and do the mundane but necessary tasks.

In the following sections, we look at some different ways to approach time management as you complete your paperwork, create schedules based on student need and teacher strength, create supervision schedules, remain visible at school events, and attend community events.

Complete Your Paperwork

One can argue that the principal's most important job is to be in classrooms and supporting teachers to be the best they can so students can achieve their potential. Next to the classroom teacher, the principal has the second largest impact on student achievement

(Robinson & Gray, 2019). Therefore, as mentioned, it is critical that the bulk of your time is focused on instructional leadership. However, you need to balance that with all the paperwork expectations that come your way.

You need to respond to people. Choose a time, perhaps before students arrive at school, to focus on email. Some responses can be quick, but some communications require further research. Respond to the individual, explaining that you need to investigate and will get back to them as soon as you can. People need to know that they are important to you and that you take their concerns seriously. Following up now, and again after you get the information you need, helps build trust.

Scheduling a face-to-face appointment with an angry parent or community member can save you some emails in the long run. Many times, people just need to tell their story. Being in classrooms regularly means you can alleviate some issues because you can speak clearly about their concerns. Teachers will love that you have their backs, and families will appreciate knowing that you are aware of what is happening in your classrooms and school.

As for district expectations, you need to ensure that you are stepping up and completing their requests. They aren't just creating work for you, but they also are responsible to their school board or the government that oversees them. If you find that they are duplicating requests from different departments, bring that to their attention, and they can streamline the process.

One district had principals create a list of all the expectations they had in their work. The district then went through the list and identified areas that they could eliminate, reduce, or that needed to continue. This was shared back to the principals, and they appreciated that their concerns were heard and addressed. Sometimes you just need to make people aware.

However, there still are many pieces that you are responsible for, so you need to find a means of handling them in a timely manner. Making a list of what is due can be very helpful (Cabeen, 2024). You will find that some items can be dealt with quickly, so do them and cross them off your list. Maybe some of the bigger items can be chunked into manageable pieces. Making progress helps one feel more in control. Is there someone who can help you complete these tasks? Do you have an assistant who can gather data or an assistant principal who can take on some of the workload? Utilize those individuals to support you.

Create Schedules Based on Student Need and Teacher Strength

Creating master schedules is a considerable task; fortunately, you typically need to do this only once or twice per school year. While one might think these schedules are simple to create, they really are much more involved. Your schedule isn't just about when and where a particular class will be; it's about ensuring the appropriate learning occurs for students because of your schedule.

Before you even begin to consider the schedule, you should connect with your teachers to understand their strengths and areas for improvement. Of course, you will have already identified a lot of this having been in classrooms regularly. However, if you're new to the school, how do you create a schedule for teachers you don't already know?

Even with a staff you are familiar with, survey them or meet with them individually to help you understand the following.

- What they teach
- What they could teach
- What they want to teach
- What they definitely don't want to teach

Sometimes you have a gem who can very capably teach a specialized subject, such as a second language, but doesn't really want to, so they've never spoken up about it. By meeting and surveying teachers, you can see what their major and minor specialties are and what they aspire to teach.

Once you've collected this data, you can begin sorting out possible combinations of classes. If you have a junior or senior high school where students choose electives, you'll want to have surveyed students as well to determine what options to offer in combination with the compulsory courses. This will already have been done if you are new to your school. This is where it becomes important to select the right teacher for the course. Is this a group of students who need extra supports?

In our experience, schedules too often have the most skilled teachers working with the higher-level courses and rookie teachers with the classes that need the most support. For instance, one of the best learning times for adolescents is mid-morning (Evans, Kelley, & Kelley, 2017) and, in our experience, right after lunch. Are we scheduling the academic courses for those time slots? Are we using existing data regarding tardies and absences? Maybe a 9:00 a.m. course that students need is better scheduled for 10:30 a.m. based on when students typically arrive at school and when the research shows is more conducive to academic achievement.

Some principals use software for this task. That can be helpful if you are able to control the variables around who is teaching what as well as ensure all times derive from your data. Whatever the case, don't just use the same schedule as the year before. For example, assume you were a second-grade teacher before becoming principal. If you taught a few periods a week in your rural K–12 school, you would likely schedule yourself into the second-grade class. However, the school's next principal may have been a secondary school teacher. If they kept the schedule from the year you were principal and didn't match their skills to the schedule, it wouldn't meet students' needs. Create every schedule for the current students and teachers.

Create Supervision Schedules

Base supervision schedules on data and the school's needs (Waterloo Catholic District School Board, 2017). What areas need the most visibility, and how do you ensure that the responsibilities are shared equitably? As mentioned earlier, it is important to include yourself on the supervision schedule. Maybe you take the morning bus supervision so you can greet all the students and their families as they enter the school. Teachers rarely complain about doing a job when they see their administrator doing the same work.

To answer those questions, familiarize yourself with the physical environment. Where are problems occurring that require closer supervision? Put a supervisor in those spots throughout daily breaks. Also, if there are outside recesses, have adequate staff outside during those times.

You can create the supervision schedule, but consider giving your staff the opportunity to work on these schedules together. They will have a critical eye that ensures everyone is doing their fair share, sometimes down to the minute. It also gives them voice and control over their time. Maybe they don't have any prep time on Thursdays, so they'd rather not supervise that day but will double up on another day when they have more time. Allowing them to create the schedule can help minimize arguments about who is or isn't doing their share.

Be Visible at Extracurricular and Curricular Events

Chapter 2 (page 15) talks about why this strategy is important to relationship and culture building. As mentioned, you don't have to take a lead role in every activity that occurs within the walls of your school, but you must be visible (Joseph, 2024). It's important for students, staff, and families to see you at these events.

Look at the school's event calendar every month. Some weeks you might be at events three or four days in a row, and then maybe your schedule levels out the week after. Put those events on your own calendar and plan accordingly.

Tips to Thrive

Ensure that all the events are not detracting from learning. Performances, special guests, and festivals are important, but you don't want students to lose too much valuable learning time.

Attend Community Events

While you want to be involved in your school's community, you can determine which events are feasible to take part in and which ones you can pass on. Sometimes, outside agencies will ask you to sit on committees or be present at their meetings. This can be valuable because you would be an advocate for your school and this may lead to the organization volunteering or donating to the school. As you ramp up your learning about how to manage your principal time in your first year or two, you will have to decide which events impact your school and students and which ones you can politely decline to attend.

Final Thoughts: Balance School and Self-Care

There are endless demands on the principal, but don't let that get you down. Honestly, the wide array of responsibilities makes the work so challenging yet so rewarding. You are the vision and culture keeper. From ensuring that learning is the key focus of the school to managing all the extra pieces that keep it running effectively, your work is all-encompassing.

Set boundaries that allow you the time and energy to run the school. All mechanisms—the budget, policies, procedures, schedules, paperwork, and problem solving—ultimately support students. Keep it as the secondary, though well-oiled, piece. Student learning must be the catalyst for all you do in your school.

Remember to schedule your time, set realistic goals, review processes to ensure efficiency, and keep an eye on staff, students, and the physical environment. To do that, you need to ensure you take care of yourself. Self-care will help you clear your head and refocus on priorities. Maybe a nature walk or a jog in the park can help you realign your thoughts. Looking after yourself is not selfish. Otherwise, you won't have the clarity or energy to deal with all that's before you.

EPILOGUE

This book is a source of both researched evidence and lived experience. We hope it provides guidance as you engage in the myriad of challenges inherent in your new role (or validates that you've handled things well in your established career). As you embark, take honest stock of your strengths, identify your growth opportunities, and reconnect with why you wanted the role.

Some well-meaning colleagues—even some friends who are not educators—may have voiced concern about the position and its responsibilities. Some may have even suggested that you've now gone to the "dark side" (moving from your teaching role into an administration role). Take this in stride. You've made the right choice, and your students, staff, school, and community will all benefit from the decision you've made. With this book as a guide, and learning for all students as the goal, your future decisions will continue to benefit all of these constituent groups.

However, remember the classic line from *Spider-Man*, when Uncle Ben reminds young Peter Parker that "with great power comes great responsibility" (Raimi, 2002). Becoming a leader should never come at the expense of remaining a learner. You have a team of talented educators, as well as support from parents and guardians and the larger community. You have students who, despite their occasional misadventures, are keen to learn and grow. All these groups will grow under your leadership, attention, passion for the role, and caring.

You were made for this!

References and Resources

Abbas, S. G., Mahjabeen, A., Ayub, U., & Iqbal, A. (2024). Examining the influence of student leadership roles on academic performance in secondary schools. *Journal for Current Sign, 2*(3), 149–162.

Ahumuza, A., & Kazaara, I. (2024). *Student leadership and its impact on behavior change in students in secondary schools.* Avance International University.

Allensworth, E. M., & Hart, H. (2018, March). *How do principals influence student achievement?* University of Chicago Consortium on School Research. Accessed at https://consortium.uchicago.edu/sites/default/files/2018-10/Leadership%20Snapshot-Mar2018-Consortium.pdf on September 15, 2025.

Alliance for Resource Equity. (n.d.). *Resource equity guidebook: Positive and inviting school climate.* Author. Accessed at https://educationresourceequity.org/wp-content/uploads/documents/dimensions/dimension-6_positive-inviting-school-climate.pdf on September 13, 2025.

American Senior High School. (n.d.). *Mission and vision.* Accessed at https://americanshs.net/mission-vision on August 4, 2025.

Anderson, S., & Rincón-Gallardo, S. (2021, June). *Learning to lead school districts effectively: A literature review.* Systems Development and Improvement Center. Accessed at https://ohioinclusiveinstructionalleadership.org/wp-content/uploads/2023/05/Anderson-Rincon-Gallardo_Lit-Review_final.pdf on May 27, 2025.

Baeder, J. (2018). *Now we're talking! 21 days to high-performance instructional leadership.* Solution Tree Press.

Bollar, S. (2025, January 2). Just do this: How to build a strong culture for the classroom, school and district. *K12 Digest.* Accessed at www.k12digest.com/just-do-this-how-to-build-a-strong-culture-for-the-classroom-school-and-district on May 27, 2025.

Bozhani, E. F., Momeni, K., & Moradi, A. (2025). The relationship between school culture and students' academic well-being through the mediating role of the satisfaction of the basic psychological needs: A correlational study. *Health Science Reports, 8*(3), Article e70379.

Cabeen, J. (2024, January 9). *5 ways to protect your time as a school leader.* Edutopia. Accessed at www.edutopia.org/article/time-management-school-administrators on May 27, 2025.

Campbell, C., Osmond-Johnson, P., Faubert, B., Zeichner, K., & Hobbs-Johnson, A. (2017). *The state of educators' professional learning in Canada: Final research report* [Conference paper]. Learning Forward. Accessed at www.researchgate.net/publication/325483416_The_State_of_Educators'_Professional_Learning_in_Canada on September 12, 2025.

Chatelain, M. (2018, October 21). We must help first-generation students master academe's "hidden curriculum". *The Chronicle of Higher Education*. Accessed at www.chronicle.com/article/we-must-help-first-generation-students-master-academes-hidden-curriculum on August 3, 2025.

Constantino, S. M. (2021). *Engage every family: Five simple principles* (2nd ed.). Corwin.

Cornell, D. (2024, August 23). *School culture: Examples, types, definition*. Accessed at https://helpfulprofessor.com/school-culture-examples-types-definition on May 27, 2025.

Covey, S. R. (2020). *The 7 habits of highly effective people* (30th anniversary ed.). Simon & Schuster.

Darling-Hammond, L., Hyler, M. E., & Gardner, M. (2017, June). *Effective teacher professional development*. Learning Policy Institute. Accessed at https://learningpolicyinstitute.org/sites/default/files/product-files/Effective_Teacher_Professional_Development_REPORT.pdf on May 27, 2025.

Darling-Hammond, L., Wechsler, M. E., Levin, S., Leung-Gagné, M., & Tozer, S. (2022, May). *Developing effective principals: What kind of learning matters?* Learning Policy Institute and the Wallace Foundation. Accessed at https://learningpolicyinstitute.org/media/3698/download?inline=&file=Developing_Effective_Principals_REPORT.pdf on August 13, 2025.

Day, C., Gu, Q., & Sammons, P. (2016). The impact of leadership on student outcomes: How successful school leaders use transformational and instructional strategies to make a difference. *Educational Administration Quarterly*, *52*(2), 221–258.

Deal, T. E., & Kennedy, A. A. (1999). *The new corporate cultures: Revitalizing the workplace after downsizing, mergers, and reeingineering*. Basic Books.

Deal, T. E., & Peterson, K. D. (2016). *Shaping school culture* (3rd ed.). Jossey-Bass.

DeWitt, P. M. (2017). *Collaborative leadership: Six influences that matter most*. Corwin.

Durham, L., Norton, L., Bird, K., & Ohlson, M. (2017). Here to stay: Supporting and empowering teachers to create a culture of consist. *The Charter Schools Research Journal*, *12*(1), 80–97.

Dweck, C. S. (2016). *Mindset: The new psychology of success*. Random House.

École Charlie Killam School. (n.d.). *Cougar code—Student behavior matrix*. Accessed at https://ckillam.brsd.ab.ca/about/student-handbook on September 8, 2025.

École Sifton School. (n.d.). *About*. Accessed at https://sifton.brsd.ab.ca/about on November 5, 2025.

Education Resource Strategies. (2017). *School design: Strategic scheduling.* Accessed at www.erstrategies.org/wp-content/uploads/2023/12/School_Design_Scheduling_Checklist.pdf on May 27, 2025.

EduSolve. (n.d.). *Best practices for principal supervision: Supporting leadership that transforms schools.* Accessed at https://edu-solve.com/best-practices-for-principal-supervision on September 8, 2025.

Epton, T., Currie, S., & Armitage, C. J. (2017). Unique effects of setting goals on behavior change: Systematic review and meta-analysis. *Journal of Consulting and Clinical Psychology, 85*(12), 1182–1198.

Evans, M. D. R., Kelley, P., & Kelley, J. (2017). Identifying the best times for cognitive functioning using new methods: Matching university times to undergraduate chronotypes. *Frontiers in Human Neuroscience, 11*, Article 188.

Farmer, D. (2025). *Oral/interpersonal communication.* WisTech Open.

Fox, E. (2021, March 23). *Developing awareness, adaptability, and flexibility as school leaders* [Blog post]. Accessed at www.nassp.org/2021/03/23/developing-awareness-adaptability-and-flexibility-as-school-leaders on May 27, 2025.

Fullan, M., & Hargreaves, A. (1996). *What's worth fighting for in your school?* Teachers College Press.

Fuller, E. J., Young, M. D., Richardson, M. S., Pendola, A., & Winn, K. M. (2018). *The pre-K–8 school leader in 2018: A 10-year study.* National Association of Elementary School Principals and University Council for Educational Administration. Accessed at www.naesp.org/resources/publications/a-10-year-study-of-the-principalship on August 15, 2025.

Gallo, A. (2023, February 15). What is psychological safety? *Harvard Business Review.* Accessed at https://hbr.org/2023/02/what-is-psychological-safety on May 27, 2025.

Goddard, R. D., Hoy, W. K., & Hoy, A. W. (2000). Collective teacher efficacy: Its meaning, measure, and impact on student achievement. *American Educational Research Journal, 37*(2), 479–507.

Gordon, J. (2017). *The power of positive leadership: How and why positive leaders transform teams and organizations and change the world.* Wiley.

Great Schools Partnership. (n.d.). *School district policies.* Accessed at www.greatschoolspartnership.org/resources/school-district-policies on May 27, 2025.

Grissom, J. A., Egalite, A. J., & Lindsay, C. A. (2021). *How principals affect students and schools: A systematic synthesis of two decades of research.* Accessed at www.wallacefoundation.org/principalsynthesis on May 27, 2025.

Gruenert, S., & Whitaker, T. (2015). *School culture rewired: How to define, assess, and transform it.* ASCD.

Hargreaves, A., & Fullan, M. (2012). *Professional capital: Transforming teaching in every school.* Teachers College Press.

Hierck, T., Coleman, C., & Weber, C. (2011). *Pyramid of behavior interventions: Seven keys to a positive learning environment.* Solution Tree Press.

Hitt, D. H., & Tucker, P. D. (2016). Systematic review of key leader practices found to influence student achievement: A unified framework. *Review of Educational Research, 86*(2), 531–569.

Hughes, J., & Morrison, L. (2022). Shifting school culture through shared leadership and support. In J. Hughes (Ed.), *Making, makers, makerspaces: The shift to making in 20 schools* (pp. 107–119). Springer.

Jackson, J. (2023). *Up to the challenge: Teaching resilience and responsibility in the classroom.* Solution Tree Press.

Jokotade, V. (2016). *Fresh start: The step-by-step journey to rebuild and renew your life.* Event House.

Joseph, M. X. (2024, February 26). *Why visible leadership is so important in K12 education.* District Administration. Accessed at https://districtadministration.com/opinion/why-visible-leadership-is-so-important-in-k12-education on May 27, 2025.

Kafele, B. K. (2019). *Is my school a better school because I lead it?* ASCD.

Kafele, B. K. (2024, April 15). *Is my school a better school because I lead it?* [Presentation]. uLead, Banff, Canada.

Kafele, B. K. (2025). *What is my value instructionally to the teachers I supervise?* ASCD.

Kouzes, J., & Posner, B. (2017). *The leadership challenge: How to make extraordinary things happen in organizations* (6th ed.). Wiley.

Le Fevre, D. (2019). *Instructional leadership and why it matters.* The Education Hub. Accessed at https://theeducationhub.org.nz/wp-content/uploads/2021/03/Instructional-leadership-and-why-it-matters.pdf on May 27, 2025.

Leithwood, K., Harris, A., & Hopkins, D. (2020). Seven strong claims about successful school leadership revisited. *School Leadership and Management, 40*(1), 5–22.

Leithwood, K., & Riehl, C. (2003). *What we know about successful school leadership.* Laboratory for Student Success, Temple University.

Levin, S., & Bradley, K. (2020). *Understanding and addressing principal turnover: A review of the research.* National Association of Secondary School Principals and Learning Policy Institute. Accessed at www.nassp.org/wp-content/uploads/2020/06/nassp_edit06-WEB.pdf on August 13, 2025.

Lim, J. R. T. (2021). Strengthening teachers' morale through awards and recognition approach. *International Journal of Research Studies in Education, 10*(9), 15–22.

Linsin, M. (2014, May 24). *Why you should avoid sending students to the principal* [Blog post]. Accessed at https://smartclassroommanagement.com/2014/05/24/why-you-should-avoid-sending-students-to-the-principal on May 27, 2025.

Mapp, K. L., & Bergman, E. (2019). *The dual capacity-building framework for family-school partnerships (version 2).* Accessed at www.dualcapacity.org on October 13, 2025.

Mapp, K. L., & Kuttner, P. J. (2013). *Partners in education: A dual capacity-building framework for family-school partnerships*. Accessed at www.ed.gov/sites/ed/files/documents/family-community/partners-education.pdf on September 15, 2025.

Marshall, P. (2025). *Today's teachers, tomorrow's leaders: A guide to identifying and developing future administrators*. Solution Tree Press.

McKibben, S. (2015, July 1). *The principal as lead learner*. Accessed at www.ascd.org/el/articles/the-principal-as-lead-learner on September 11, 2025.

Merrigan, R. (2024, August 5). *5 tips for learning students' names*. Edutopia. Accessed at www.edutopia.org/article/tips-learning-students-names on August 28, 2025.

Mormah, F. O. (2023). The management and maintenance of physical facilities for quality assurance in higher education in the 21st century with innovative technologies. *African Educational Research Journal, 11*(2), 220–224.

Morrell, M., & Capparell, S. (2001). *Shackleton's way: Leadership lessons from the great Antarctic explorer*. Viking.

Muhammad, A. (2024). *The way forward: PLC at Work and the bright future of education*. Solution Tree Press.

Muir, T. (2023, October 5). *The reality of school staff conflict* [Blog post]. Accessed at www.trevormuir.com/blog/school-staff-conflict on May 27, 2025.

Murray, T. (2025, August 9). *Building a positive school culture* [Blog post]. Accessed at www.thomascmurray.com/blog/building-a-positive-school-culture on November 24, 2025.

Nellie McClung School. (n.d.). *Our school*. Accessed at https://nelliemcclung.cbe.ab.ca/school on August 4, 2025.

New Leaders. (n.d.). *Distributed leadership: Why the right time is now* [Blog post]. Accessed at www.newleaders.org/blog/distributed-leadership-why-the-right-time-is-right-now on September 12, 2025.

Nowak, A., Biesaga, M., Ziembowicz, K., Baran, T., & Winkielman, P. (2023). Subjective consistency increases trust. *Scientific Reports, 13*, Article 5657.

Ontario Ministry of Education. (2012). *Setting goals: The power of purpose—Exploring five core leadership capacities* (Bulletin No. 4). Accessed at www.sgdsb.on.ca/upload/documents/blds---iia-4---setting-goals.pdf on February 2, 2025.

Ostovar-Nameghi, S. A., & Sheikhahmadi, M. (2016). From teacher isolation to teacher collaboration: Theoretical perspectives and empirical findings. *English Language Teaching, 9*(5), 197–205.

Patil, M., Biswas, S., & Kaur, R. (2019). Does gratitude impact employee morale in the workplace. *Journal of Applied Management, 10*(2), 21–36.

Pearson, P. L. (2015). *High school culture, graduation rates, and dropout rates* [Doctoral dissertation, University of Southern Mississippi]. The Aquila Digital Community. https://aquila.usm.edu/cgi/viewcontent.cgi?params=/context/dissertations/article/1063/&path_info=auto_convert.pdf

Prendergast, L., & Lee, P. (2024). *Habits of resilient educators: Strategies for thriving during times of anxiety, doubt, and constant change*. Corwin.

Price, H. E., & Moolenaar, N. M. (2015). Principal-teacher relationships: Foregrounding the international importance of principals' social relationships for school learning climates. *Journal of Educational Administration*, *53*(1).

Raimi, S. (Director). (2002). *Spider-Man* [Film]. Columbia Pictures; Marvel Enterprises; Lara Ziskin Productions.

Ratanjee, V. (2022, June 14). *How to build trust in the workplace*. Accessed at www.gallup.com/workplace/393401/trust-decline-rebuild.aspx on August 3, 2025.

Regional Educational Laboratory. (2021, June). *Engaging families to support students' connectedness to school*. WestEd. Accessed at https://ies.ed.gov/sites/default/files/migrated/rel/regions/west/relwestFiles/pdf/4-2-3-22_Engaging_Families_to_Support_Students_Connectedness_to_School_508.pdf on September 10, 2025.

Ribeiro, L. M. C., Mamede, S., de Brito, E. M., Moura, A. S., de Faria, R. M. D., & Schmidt, H. G. (2019). *Effects of deliberate reflection on students' engagement in learning and learning outcomes* [Abstract]. Accessed at https://asmepublications.onlinelibrary.wiley.com/doi/abs/10.1111/medu.13798 on August 13, 2025.

Robinson, V. (2011). *Student-centered leadership*. Jossey-Bass.

Robinson, V. (2023). *Virtuous educational leadership: Doing the right work the right way*. Corwin.

Robinson, V., & Gray, E. (2019). What difference does school leadership make to student outcomes? *Journal of the Royal Society of New Zealand*, *49*(2), 171–187. https://doi.org/10.1080/03036758.2019.1582075

Roghanizad, M., & Bohns, V. (2021, December 20). *Need a favor? Research suggests it's best to ask in person*. Harvard Business Review. Accessed at https://hbr.org/2021/12/need-a-favor-research-suggests-its-best-to-ask-in-person on September 13, 2025.

SaferWatch. (2023). *Preparation is key: Essential school drills and exercises for 2023* [Blog post]. Accessed at www.saferwatchapp.com/blog/school-drills-exercises on May 27, 2025.

Samuels, C. A. (2019, October 15). What principals can do when parents and teachers clash. *Education Week*. Accessed at www.edweek.org/leadership/what-principals-can-do-when-parents-and-teachers-clash/2019/10 on September 12, 2025.

Schneider, B. (2003). *Trust in schools: A core resource for school reform*. Accessed at www.ascd.org/el/articles/trust-in-schools-a-core-resource-for-school-reform on September 12, 2025.

Schneider, E. J., & Hollenczer, L. L. (2006). *The principal's guide to managing communication*. Corwin.

Scott, S. (2002). *Fierce conversations: Achieving success at work and in life one conversation at a time*. Berkley.

Shafer, L. (2018, July 23). *What makes a good school culture?* Accessed at www.gse.harvard.edu/ideas/usable-knowledge/18/07/what-makes-good-school-culture on February 25, 2025.

Sinek, S. (2009). *Start with why: How great leaders inspire everyone to take action.* Portfolio.

Solomon, E. (2025, February 5). The alpha leadership lie. *Psychology Today.* Accessed at www.psychologytoday.com/us/blog/story-over-spreadsheet/202502/the-alpha-leadership-lie on May 27, 2025.

State of Oregon. (n.d.). *6 types of school cultures—Brief descriptions.* Accessed at www.oregon.gov/ode/schools-and-districts/grants/mentoring/Documents/bamrt4_SchoolCultureDescriptions.docx on February 22, 2025.

Stewart-Banks, B., Kuofie, M., Hakim, A., & Branch, R. (2015). Education leadership styles impact on work performance and morale of staff. *Journal of Marketing and Management, 6*(2), 87–105.

Stoll, L. (n.d.). *School culture.* Accessed at www.educationalleaders.govt.nz/Culture/Leading-cultural-change/School-culture on May 27, 2025.

Superville, D. R. (2019, September 24). For already burdened principals, budget control remains elusive. *Education Week.* Accessed at www.edweek.org/leadership/for-already-burdened-principals-budget-control-remains-elusive/2019/09 on May 27, 2025.

Thomas, C., Turner, J., Koehn, J., Brandon, J., Friesen, S., Marler, R., et al. (2021, August 31). *Addressing Alberta's new leadership quality standard through high quality collaborative professional learning.* Accessed at https://jamconsulting.ca/wp-content/uploads/2023/04/addressing-albertas-new-leadership-quality-standard-through-high-quality-collaborative-professional-learning.pdf on September 11, 2025.

Torres, D. G. (2019). Distributed leadership, professional collaboration, and teachers' job satisfaction in U.S. schools. *Teaching and Teacher Education, 79,* 111–123.

University of Massachusetts Global. (2020, April 1). *How to create school vision statements that lead to long-term success* [Blog post]. Accessed at www.umassglobal.edu/blog-news/how-to-create-school-vision-statements-that-lead-to-long-term-success on September 13, 2025.

Waterloo Catholic District School Board. (2017). *Step 6: Build a supervision plan.* Author. Accessed at www.wcdsb.ca/wp-content/uploads/sites/36/2017/02/PartC.pdf on May 27, 2025.

Wells, L. (2023, October 24). *6 things principals can focus on to improve family engagement* [Blog post]. Accessed at www.nwea.org/blog/2023/6-things-principals-can-focus-on-to-improve-family-engagement on September 13, 2025.

Wetaskiwin Regional Public Schools. (n.d.). *Falun Elementary School.* Accessed at www.wrps11.ca/schools/our-schools/141 on August 4, 2025.

Williams, K. C., & Hierck, T. (2015). *Starting a movement: Building culture from the inside out in professional learning communities.* Solution Tree Press.

Wilson, S. (n.d.). *What is school culture?* Accessed at www.educationalleadershipdegree.com/frequently-asked-questions/what-is-school-culture on May 27, 2025.

Winemiller, S. M. (2019). *Exploring the principal-assistant principal relationship to discover principal practices influencing the assistant principal's instructional leadership: A case study* [Doctoral dissertation, Drexel University]. Drexel University Libraries. https://researchdiscovery.drexel.edu/esploro/outputs/doctoral/Exploring-the-Principal-Assistant-Principal-Relationship-to/991014632381304721

Yoestara, M., Putri, Z., & Ismail, N. M. (2020). School appreciation and teachers' competence: Are they correlated? *International Journal of Language Studies, 14*(3), 47–66.

Young, P. G. (2023, July 27). *Finding and hiring the right teachers for your school.* Edutopia. Accessed at www.edutopia.org/article/questions-school-leaders-can-use-hire-teachers on August 30, 2025.

Zulqarnain, M., Ali, V., & Bashir, I. (2025). Effect of school culture on teachers' burnout and job performance at elementary level. *Pakistan Languages and Humanities Review, 9*(3), 134–146.

Index

H

I

J

K

L

M

You're a Teacher Now! What's Next?
Tom Hierck and Alex Kajitani
Trusted education experts Tom Hierck and Alex Kajitani draw from their experiences to offer research-backed tools and strategies in an easily referenced FAQ format that both new and veteran teachers can use in their classrooms to address everything from behavior management to self-care planning.
BKG142

Trauma-Sensitive Leadership
John F. Eller and Tom Hierck
Lead a foundational shift in the way your school approaches student behavior. Using straightforward language, the authors offer research-based, practical strategies for understanding and supporting trauma-impacted students and providing a safe environment for them to learn.
BKF911

What Are You Bringing to the Potluck?
Sheldon L. Eakins
Through personal stories and practical tools, Sheldon L. Eakins serves up ways to change attitudes and behaviors that lead to exclusion. He offers leaders a way through their potential fears and the ingredients to create a supportive community that encourages empathy for all students.
BKG248

Finding Your Balance
Joshua Ray
Drawing on personal experiences, author Joshua Ray offers practical strategies, relatable anecdotes, and templates to help leaders thrive personally and professionally. Learn to prioritize work-life balance, overcome impostor syndrome, and lead intentionally, while discovering wellness strategies that help leaders be effective and efficient.
BKG250

Visit SolutionTree.com or call 800.733.6786 to order.

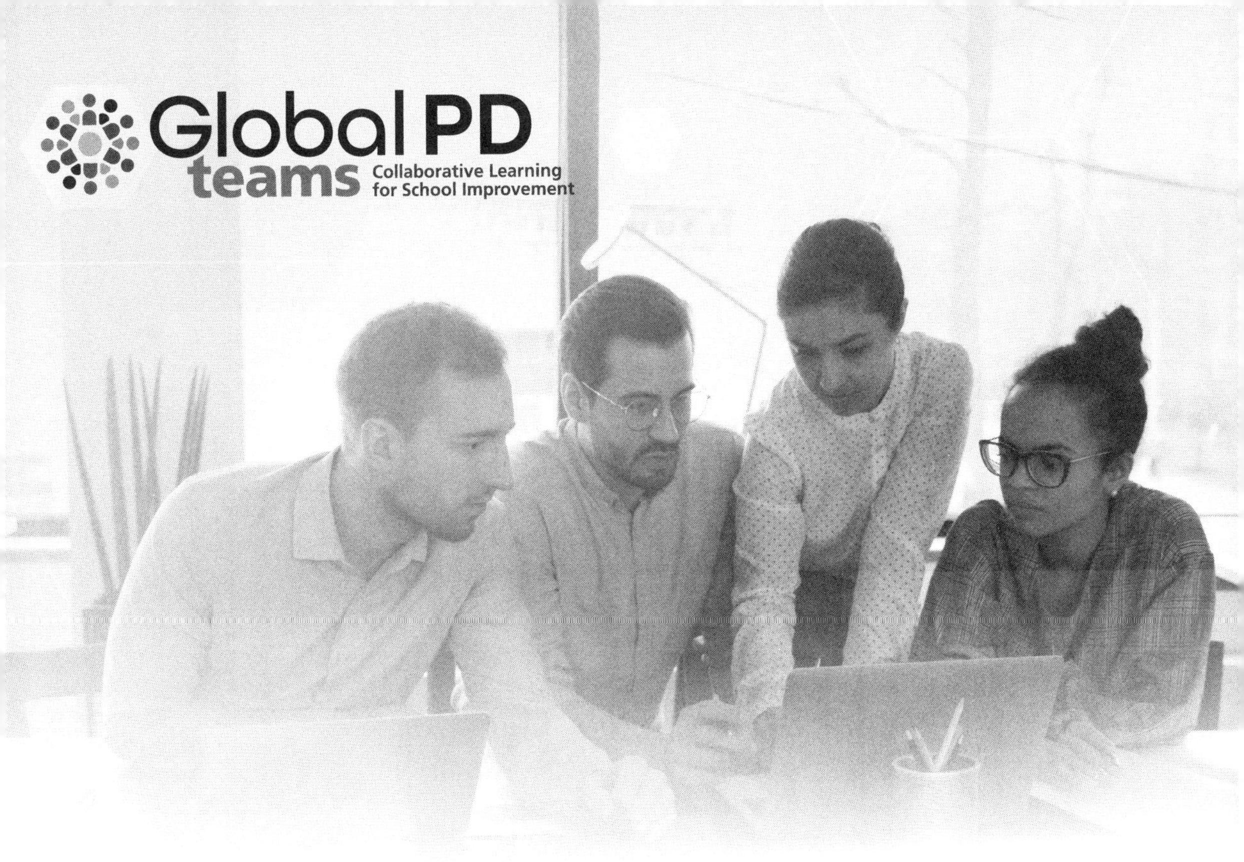
Global PD
teams
Collaborative Learning
for School Improvement